About the Author

BERNARD GOLDBERG is the number one *New York Times* bestselling author of *Bias*, *100 People Who Are Screwing Up America*, and *Arrogance*. He has won eight Emmy Awards for his work at CBS News and at HBO, where he now reports for the acclaimed program *Real Sports*. In 2006 he won the Alfred I. duPont–Columbia University Award, the most prestigious of all broadcast journalism awards.

CRAZIES
TO THE LEFT
OF ME,
WIMPS
TO THE RIGHT

Also by Bernard Goldberg

Bias: A CBS Insider Exposes
How the Media Distort the News

Arrogance: Rescuing America from the Media Elite

100 People Who Are Screwing Up America
(and Al Franken Is #37)

CRAZIES TO THE LEFT OF ME, WIMPS TO THE RIGHT

HOW ONE SIDE LOST ITS MIND AND THE OTHER LOST ITS NERVE

★ ★ ★ ★ ★ ★ ★ ★ ★ ★ ★ ★ ★

BERNARD GOLDBERG

HARPER

NEW YORK • LONDON • TORONTO • SYDNEY

HARPER

A hardcover edition of this book was published in 2007 by Harper-Collins Publishers.

FIRST HARPER PAPERBACK PUBLISHED 2008.

Designed by Emily Cavett Taff

Library of Congress Cataloging-in-Publication Data is available upon request.

ISBN 978-0-06-125258-7 (pbk.)

08 09 10 11 12 ID/RRD 10 9 8 7 6 5 4 3 2 1

This one's for Mom,
*who went peacefully on
Thanksgiving morning 2006 at ninety-one*

Contents

Contents

**Just What We Need: A City with
Rice-A-Roni *and* a Foreign Policy . . .
and Four Other Reasons Liberals
Are Even Crazier Than We Thought**

**How the Religious Right
(and the Loony Left) Turned
Barry Goldwater into a Liberal**

**Being Liberal Means Never
Having to Say You're Sorry**

**Donkeys to the Left of Me ...
Pigs to the Right**

**Islam Is a Religion of Peace, and
If You Don't Believe Me I'll Kill You**

**All the News That Fits
Their Ideology (Part 1)**

We Don't Need No Stinking Principles

CRAZIES
TO THE **LEFT**
OF ME,
WIMP'S
TO THE **RIGHT**

★ ★ ★ ★ ★ ★ ★ ★ ★ ★ ★

Just My Luck: I'm on One Side and They Lose Their Minds ... I Go to the Other Side and They Lose Their Cojones

Crazies to
the Left of Me...

When I was growing up in the Bronx in the
1950s, I didn't know about liberals or conservatives. But I did know
about the New York Yankees.

The Yanks were my life back then. Sometimes when they'd lose,
which was almost never, I would stop eating. When I was ten years
old, I was the Mahatma Gandhi of the Bronx. Gandhi fasted for
long stretches in order to change an oppressive social order. I fasted
for maybe a day until Mickey or Yogi or one of the other Bronx
Bombers knocked one out of the park and the Yankees won again.
In both cases, going without food highlighted a terrible injustice,
and in the end our sacrifices made the world a better place.

Back then, the Yankees' many critics (most of them sore losers
from Brooklyn) would say that rooting for the Yanks was like rooting for General Motors. As a kid I didn't quite grasp the meaning,
but I knew it wasn't good. General Motors was big business, the
embodiment of corporate power. GM was—forgive my language—
Republican!

Which meant the tycoons who ran General Motors went to
snooty country clubs and ate expensive meals at fancy restaurants.
We hung out on the roof of the tenement—a place we called "tar
beach"—and ate at diners; that is, on those rare occasions when
we ate out at all. Republicans didn't represent us. We were Democrats. And I can honestly say that during my entire childhood in the

Bronx, I never met even one Republican there. Not one. Frankly, I don't think they existed.

The Democrats were for the "working man," just like my father, who got up before dawn every day and headed off to a factory where he ran big, clanking machines that put embroidery on dresses and tablecloths and just about anything else. He worked hard and although he never made a lot of money he always took care of his family. He and all the others like him were the blue-collar backbone of the Democratic Party.

None of the men I knew growing up had white-collar jobs. They all worked in factories, like my father did, or in little dry-goods stores selling hats and coats, or in garages fixing cars. The women stayed home and took care of the kids. None of them had jobs outside the house. That would have reflected badly on their husbands, an indication that the man of the house couldn't provide for his own family. None of the grown-ups had gone to college. Most of them hadn't even finished high school, which wasn't the least bit unusual in those days. Their savior was Franklin Delano Roosevelt, who got them through the dark days of the Great Depression. FDR, because of his polio, could hardly move without a wheelchair. But to the faithful where I grew up, he could walk on water.

So, it's not exactly a mystery why years later, when my interests extended beyond Yankee Stadium, I took the road my parents had traveled and became a Democrat. I didn't even have to think about it. It's just who I was. Up North we were all liberal Democrats, of course, but on the news we heard about the other kind of Democrat, who lived in the South, the conservative kind. But in those days no decent person, certainly not after the civil rights movement began, would get caught so much as washing his hands in the same sink as a conservative. They were not like us. They were bigots and cowards who had to hide behind a flimsy excuse they called states' rights, and the muscle of nasty sheriffs, to hang on to a way of life that struck many of us as not worth hanging on to. I despised conservatives back then.

In the early '60s, when I was still in high school, we took our first long family road trip south, to visit relatives in faraway, exotic Florida. We traveled in my dad's prized possession, a two-tone, black and white, 1954 Plymouth, which he would polish with an old rag every chance he got. Someplace in the South—Virginia, or one of the Carolinas maybe—we pulled into an old, wooden roadside restaurant for lunch. This was still the Old South, remember, and before we even got out of the car, I saw the sign, one I had only seen before on television and in the newspaper. NO COLOREDS ALLOWED, it said.

My parents weren't bigots. They were appalled, like decent people everywhere, when they watched the news and saw Bull Connor sending his dogs after civil rights marchers, or state troopers beating black people with nightsticks just because they wanted the same rights as everyone else had in America. And they even knew, I suspect, that the same kind of people who didn't want blacks in their restaurant didn't want our kind—Jews—in there, either. But my parents were of a certain generation, and so they were willing to accommodate the bigotry—or at least turn a blind eye—in order to get a sandwich, a soda, and get the hell out of there.

They didn't want to rock the boat. I, on the other hand, at seventeen, wanted to sink the damn thing with every last racist son of a bitch in it. So I told my folks that I would wait in the car while they and my little brother went inside to eat. But, as it turned out, they decided not to go in, either. And before you could say "Jim Crow," we were back on the highway heading south.

It was exciting to be a liberal in the 1960s. America was changing and we were on the right side, the side of equality and decency and fair play. That's what the country was about, wasn't it? Being a liberal back then made me proud. Conservatives, on the other hand, were on the wrong side of history. They were an embarrassment.

★

I was the first person in my family to go to college. I went to Rutgers University, in New Brunswick, New Jersey—a school that opened its doors in 1766, ten years before there even was a United States. It was the first time I had stepped out of the narrow confines of the Bronx, or of the small, blue-collar town in New Jersey, Bergenfield, where we had moved in the summer of 1960. It was the first time I really began to understand that the world was a bigger place than anything I had known.

During a bull session at the dorm one night, several of my pals and I decided, with typical college-boy bravado, that we would leave the country and move to Australia if Barry Goldwater won the presidency in 1964. The guy was just plain scary. If he could, we figured, he'd blow up everybody in North Vietnam, and that was just for openers. Then he'd find commie bastards someplace else to drop a few nukes on. And if that wasn't bad enough, he, like all the other Neanderthals, was against the new civil rights laws. Who in his right mind was against civil rights? No way were we staying if this screwball won.

Fortunately, he didn't win and we didn't have to leave. But looking back, this was an early warning about how intolerant liberals—including my youthful self—could be. What we really were saying was that we not only knew better but that we *were* better. If Americans were so dumb that they actually would elect this conservative from out West, then it was time for us to go. We were acting like morons, of course, too young and too sanctimonious to know it. We were the forerunners of all those adult sanctimonious morons who make up the Hollywood glitzocracy and who threatened to leave the country if George W. Bush was elected, but of course didn't.

After college I kept my liberal credentials in impeccable order by voting for Hubert Humphrey in 1968, George McGovern in 1972, and Jimmy Carter in 1976. But looking back, I realize I was just going through the motions. My vote for Humphrey made sense. But by 1972, the Democrats were changing in some fundamental ways. They were becoming elitists—the very kind of people we used to detest back in the old neighborhood. And the fact that they were *liberal* elitists didn't make it any more palatable.

Thanks to the so-called McGovern Revolution, affluent, well-educated liberals were in—the "new elite," as one newspaper called them—and blue-collar Democrats were out. I remember hearing that at the 1972 Democratic National Convention, New York had only three union members as delegates (out of about two hundred), but at least nine delegates who represented the gay liberation movement. The Iowa delegation, incredibly, had no farmers. Thirty-nine percent of the convention delegates had attended graduate school. More than a third of the white delegates identified themselves as secularists, compared with only 5 percent of the general population. De facto quotas were set up to bring more women and minority delegates in. This prompted two New York City journalists—Jack Newfield and Joe Flaherty, both McGovern supporters who came from working-class backgrounds—to ask the politically incorrect question: Where were the quotas for the Irish, Italians, and Poles? All of a sudden, the biggest domestic issues on the Democratic agenda were gay rights, abortion, and hard-edged feminism. This wasn't a party so much of liberals anymore; it was a party of leftists. And it definitely wasn't my father's Democratic Party.

It all started, I guess, with Vietnam. That's when liberalism took a hard left turn. It wasn't enough for liberals simply to protest against the war. No, they had to demonize our own military. You heard stories about how soldiers were spit on when they came home from Vietnam. To the hard Left—a force that was taking control of the liberal movement in the country—*America* was corrupt! It's one thing to be against the war. But something else altogether to be against your own country. I just couldn't buy into that.

I had trouble buying into the new feminism movement, too. Sure I was for equality and fairness. But like the antiwar liberals, the new feminists were shrill, angry, and intolerant. It wasn't enough to support equal pay for equal work. It wasn't enough to say, "Sure, women should have all the same opportunities that men have." Now you had to believe that men were the enemy—the *patriarchal oppressors*. Feminism may have started out as a noble civil rights movement but the man-haters who were in charge turned it into a nasty little package of resentments. It became nothing less than an all-out war on biology. So what if a woman wasn't strong enough to carry a man out of a burning building, feminists demanded to know. Women had the *right* to be firefighters, damn it, just like men! I needed that kind of crap like a fish needs a bicycle.

★

The country was in turmoil, and I guess I was too. Liberals—the new kind, anyway—were angry. Everything was about grievances. They were becoming closed-minded and orthodox. They were forgetting how to be liberal.

In 2005, Noemie Emery, who writes brilliantly about politics and American culture, made this observation in the *Weekly Standard* about how the national Democratic Party, the liberal party in America, had lost its way: "The Democrats who used to produce things—cars, steel, and foodstuffs—are being replaced by those who produce fads and fashions, things people enjoy but don't need. Societies need teachers, soldiers, engineers, and mechanics; they need people who drill for oil and fix cars; people who understand war and politics. No one needs sitcoms, movie reviews, handbag designers, gossip columnists, or professors of gender construction, but this superfluous cadre is becoming the core of the party of Truman and Roosevelt, an alliance of the superficial and trivial, along with the hopelessly poor. Call it the FDR coalition, minus the South, minus the farmers, minus a large part of labor, which has been weakening, and seeing the nonpublic sector part of its membership go over to voting Republican. This is not a national coalition, but it does know the best stores and best restaurants, and knows where to go for good hair."

In other words, these new, trendy Democrats wouldn't have lasted ten minutes in my old Bronx neighborhood. Somebody would have kicked their asses—as a matter of principle. They were soft and glitzy and they were making my head spin. I felt like Butch Cassidy, who kept wondering: "Who *are* those guys?" And of all the things my dear old blue-collar dad cared about in the whole wide world, finding the "best restaurants" or fretting over where to go for "good hair" (he was bald!) weren't anywhere on his list. He didn't recognize the party he had been so loyal to.

★

Even as a kid in junior high school in the Bronx, I wanted to be a newsman. There were no journalists in my family. I didn't know any personally. But I did read about the Yankees every day in the *Daily News* and I think that's where I caught the bug. Covering baseball and football, I thought, would be exciting. But as I got older, I figured you can't sit at the grown-up table if you cover sports. So I decided instead to be a "real" reporter, and right out of college, in 1967, I went to work at the Associated Press in New York, earning the princely sum of $102.50 a week, which wasn't a lot even back then. After a few years of poverty and one winter snowstorm too many, I moved to Miami and got a job in local television, where I first met the CBS News White House correspondent—a fellow named Dan Rather. And then, in 1972, I got a call from the big leagues. CBS News wanted me to join the team.

My first big assignment that year was covering the McGovern campaign behind the scenes as a producer. I was still in my twenties and couldn't believe how lucky I was. *I was working for CBS News!* I still wasn't getting paid much ($17,000 and change to start), but I would have worked for free. I no longer was simply Bernard Goldberg. Now, whenever I introduced myself, I was "Bernard Goldberg, CBS News." CBS News was part of who I was.

I was based in Atlanta when I started, and I was meeting all kinds of fascinating people. Some influenced history, like Jimmy Carter and George Wallace. Some made America better by fighting for civil rights—people like Andrew Young and Martin Luther King Senior, "Daddy King" as he was known. I interviewed the Watergate burglars in Miami and reported on the Boy in the Bubble at a hospital in Houston. I was in Managua, Nicaragua, just hours after an earthquake devastated the city. I even shook hands with Pope John Paul II at the Vatican. I loved being part of the news organization that Ed Murrow had made famous. Now I was working for Walter Cronkite and alongside guys like Charles Kuralt, Roger Mudd, and the very same Dan Rather I had met a few years earlier in Miami. Not bad for a kid from the Bronx. What a country, huh?

In 1981, after a few years at the CBS News bureau in San Francisco, I moved to the network's headquarters in New York. And that's when everything changed. That's when I began to see for myself just how closed-minded my liberal colleagues were—and how biased, too.

The first thing I noticed was that a lot of reporters would put a liberal slant on many of the important stories we put on the air, whether they were about race, feminism, homelessness, or AIDS. We ran hyped-up programs about how a deadly epidemic of HIV was going to spread to the white, middle-class, heterosexual sub-urbs of America. Setting aside our usual skepticism, we ran with the story—because the gay activists told us it was true, and they wouldn't lie, would they?

Well, yes. They used the media to scare the hell out of America, figuring it was the only way to get Washington to come up with money to fight the disease. This was a case of very bad journalism, but the media gladly went right along with the story. Why? Because liberals love to root for the underdog. It makes them feel noble. Never mind that we were being used by activists with an agenda. If it were "gun nuts" in the National Rifle Association trying to spin us, we would have told them to take a hike. But that's not how liberals deal with the people they like. So we passed along every scary story the AIDS lobby fed us, and in the process we spread an epidemic of fear throughout the country—and never once apologized for being such willing dupes.

We ran tons of stories about the homeless when Ronald Reagan was in the White House, but only a few when Jimmy Carter and Bill Clinton were presidents. The message was clear: Democrats are the good ones, the decent ones. They're the ones who take care of poor people. Republicans are the uncaring monsters who leave the poor to starve in the streets. Our agenda, in short, was the liberal agenda.

★

Nineteen-eighty was a big year for me. I was done with the Democrats by then but couldn't yet bring myself to cross the Rubicon and go Republican. Throughout the '80s, I was, as they say, in transition. But even though I didn't vote for Reagan—not in 1980 or 1984—I liked his good humor and a lot of what he stood for. I had never so much as flirted with Republicans before, but here was a guy who appealed to my common sense.

I couldn't figure out why, for example, liberals went nuts every time he uttered the words "evil empire." Wasn't that exactly what the Soviet Union was? The ruthless old guys in the Kremlin had no respect for traditional liberal values like free speech or tolerance of dissent. Disagree with the state and they'd put your dissident rear end on a train to Siberia or toss it into a gulag in some godforsaken corner of the earth. What liberals didn't seem to understand was that the Soviet Union wasn't simply a threat to the United States of America. It also was a threat to American liberalism, to the very values that American liberals deeply believed in.

I also liked the fact that Reagan cut taxes. Yes, my taxes. During the Reagan years I kept thinking that Democrats loved me when I was making next to nothing and paying almost no taxes to support their many well-intentioned but often useless social programs, like welfare for people who had absolutely no interest in ever getting a job. But now that I was doing considerably better, I—and all the others like me—became the Democrats' piñata. Suddenly we were villains who weren't paying our "fair share."

This was also a time when I was beginning to see the depth and power of white liberal guilt and how it would turn liberalism on its head. Affirmative action, after all, is just about the most *illiberal* program going. It isn't about judging someone by the content of his character. It's about judging people by the color of their skin. Exactly the opposite of what Martin Luther King had fought for. Back in the '60s I would have needed a crystal ball to see how my liberal friends, who talked endlessly about their dream of a "color-blind America," would soon find all sorts of devious ways to bring color into almost every important decision they made, whether it was about whom to let into college or whom to hire for a job.

For years I had thought the Democratic Party was in my DNA. But now I understood it was nurture, not nature that had kept me with them for so long. I was getting older and, hopefully, wiser. I had seen a lot more than the Bronx and Bergenfield. I was adapting to a new political reality and because of all that, I was slowly but inevitably moving to the right.

★

By the mid-'90s, after many years of complaining in private at CBS News, I had had enough of the bias and decided to express my disdain in a public forum. In 1996, I wrote an op-ed for the *Wall Street Journal* about how the networks routinely slant the news to the left. I started out by saying, "There are lots of reasons fewer and fewer people are watching network news, and one of them, I'm more convinced than ever, is that our viewers simply don't trust us. And for good reason."

Then I uttered the magic words: liberal bias.

"The old argument that the networks and other 'media elites' have a liberal bias is so blatantly true that it's hardly worth discussing anymore. No, we don't sit around in dark corners and plan strategies on how we're going to slant the news. We don't have to. It comes naturally to most reporters."

Foolishly, I thought the op-ed might touch off an important debate in the news industry. The subject was so important, I figured, how could it not? Boy was I wrong! About two seconds after the op-ed was published, I got my first big, very personal lesson in how intolerant those "tolerant" liberals could be. Some of my colleagues were calling me a "traitor," which I found amusing since these were the kinds of liberals who wouldn't call a real traitor a traitor (like those "idealistic" Americans who leave their comfy homes in the suburbs, move to Afghanistan, and join the Taliban). Others thought I should be fired outright for expressing such a *deviant* opinion. I did stray, after all, from the liberal-media plantation. And that made all those supposedly open-minded liberal journalists at CBS News very, very mad.

But in reality these were liberals—or "progressives," as they started calling themselves—who were neither liberal nor progressive. They were the new media elite—big, powerful, and hopelessly out of touch with most of the people who live between the Upper West Side of Manhattan and Beverly Hills. These are not people who want debate, no matter how much they say they do. They want orthodoxy; their liberal orthodoxy, imposed on the rest of us.

★

I left CBS News in July 2000, after I got turned down for a job on the new *60 Minutes* weekday program—more punishment, I figured, for my op-ed about liberal bias. That's when I wrote my first book, *Bias*, a firsthand, behind-the-scenes account of how liberals in America's most important newsrooms slant the news. Naturally, I couldn't find a publisher in Manhattan to touch it. Ten seconds before throwing in the towel, I took the manuscript to a small conservative outfit in Washington, called Regnery, which enthusiastically published the book. It quickly became a *New York Times* number-one bestseller. While liberal publishers in New York couldn't understand for the life of them who would want to read my book, *Bias* resonated with ordinary Americans who were fed up with the elite liberal mentality that dominated the networks and America's most powerful newspapers.

The book came out three months after the attacks on America on September 11, 2001, a turning point for the nation and for me personally. That's when my break with the Left, which had been a long time coming, was complete. Finally and officially, I crossed over to the other side.

Liberals—not all of them, to be sure, but way too many of the educated and Hollywood elite—couldn't wait to blame America for what happened that day. A professor at my old alma mater, Rutgers, sent an e-mail to her students, saying, "We should be aware that, whatever its proximate cause, its ultimate cause is the fascism of the United States foreign policy over the past many decades." Another professor, this one at Columbia, said, "I'm not sure which is more frightening—the horror that engulfed New York City or the apocalyptic rhetoric emanating daily from the White House." Even screwball teachers at major American universities banded together to announce that the attack on 9/11 was an "inside job" orchestrated by people in the Bush administration to provide the president with an excuse to go to war for oil in the Middle East before moving on to bigger things, like world domination.

Katha Pollitt, the liberal writer whose work appears in many left-of-center publications, wrote a piece for the *Nation* magazine, which opened with, "My daughter who goes to Stuyvesant High School only blocks from the World Trade Center thinks we should fly an American flag out our window. Definitely not, I say: The flag stands for jingoism and vengeance and war."

And since 9/11, the rhetoric has only gotten worse. In Hollywood, there has been more visceral anger directed at George Bush than at Osama bin Laden. Harry Belafonte called President Bush "the greatest tyrant in the world, the greatest terrorist in the world." John Mellencamp said the president was "a cheap thug." Chevy Chase, at a gala at the Kennedy Center in Washington, told a packed house that George Bush was a "dumb f**k." Others were content simply calling him a Nazi.

I felt the same toxins closer to home, too. When that British movie came out, about the assassination of President Bush, I conducted a little experiment. I asked a guy I play basketball with in Miami—his name is Robert and he's a true-blue liberal, originally from Massachusetts—whether he thought it would be a good idea if George Bush were *really* assassinated. Robert is a bright guy, a businessman, who, the best I can figure, is fairly rational—except when the conversation turns to Public Enemy Number One, George W. Bush.

"So what do you think, Robert?" I asked. "Good idea or bad idea that somebody *actually* kill President Bush?"

Frankly, I figured he'd smirk and walk away. Instead, he actually thought about the question I had just asked him. In fact, he thought about it for a very long time. It was probably only twenty seconds or so, but it seemed like an hour and a half before he finally said, "Probably a bad idea," pronouncing the word "probably" very slowly and in a voice indicating he wasn't all that convinced it was such a bad idea.

"Why?" I asked him. "Why only *probably*?"

"Because I don't want him to be president," he said, as if the answer was obvious.

"You know there are other ways to get rid of a president. Ever hear of an *election*?" I said.

"We had one of those back in 2000," he quickly replied, "and they stole it!"

★

Liberals weren't always that dark and cynical. They weren't like that after Pearl Harbor. Back then *all* Americans knew who the enemy was—and it wasn't Franklin Roosevelt. Today, the "new elite"—the activist base of the Democratic Party—is angry. Their hatred of George W. Bush has pushed many of them over the edge. They have become deranged. In fact, if you want to understand contemporary liberal thinking, you need to know just one simple, easy-to-remember fact: George W. Bush is responsible for everything bad that happens anyplace in the country, in the world, or in the whole damn universe! That pretty much sums it up. So they blame him, and America, for whatever they don't like. Many of them simply don't believe America is a good country anymore.

And in case you think that's a low blow, a slanderous characterization of today's liberals, consider this: In 2004, Scott Rasmussen, the pollster, asked one thousand "likely voters" two questions about the nature of America: Is this country generally fair and decent? Would the world be better off if more countries were more like America? Just over 80 percent of Bush voters answered yes to both questions. Just under 50 percent of John Kerry voters said yes. As Michael Barone, the political analyst, put it, "That's reminiscent of the story about the Teamsters Union business agent who was in the hospital and received a bouquet of flowers with a note that read, 'The executive board wishes you a speedy recovery by a vote of 9–6.' Not exactly a wholehearted endorsement."

This kind of thinking, this unwillingness by so many liberals to endorse the notion of America's basic decency, is setting liberalism back fifty years. Which, when you think about it, might actually be a good thing. Fifty years ago, liberalism was something to be proud of. Today, nothing about the liberal landscape seems familiar. The terrain is unrecognizable. I have a feeling, Toto, we're not in the Bronx anymore.

Wimps to
the Right...

My liberal friends think I've gone over to the Dark Side. They don't understand how I could be "one of *them*." They say "them" as if it were a disease.

Sometimes they just laugh. "Come on," they say, "you're not *really* a conservative." The whole idea strikes them as preposterous, too crazy to be taken seriously. After all, they figure, I'm not a racist. I can read and write. I'm not married to my sister. And I don't drool on myself. So how in the world could I possibly be a conservative?

Good thing liberals are open-minded and hate stereotyping.

The fact is that we no longer speak the same language, liberals and conservatives. We don't listen to each other. We have different facts, which we use to come to different conclusions. Maybe it's always been like this, but it feels worse now than ever. My perceptive pal Burt Prelutsky summed it up this way: "Conservatives are from Mars; liberals are from San Francisco."

I once tried to explain to a liberal colleague at CBS News why the state of American culture mattered so much to conservatives. I told him that conservatives felt the culture was getting too raunchy; that violent rap music and juvenile sex jokes on early-evening TV sitcoms were a form of air pollution. I tried to explain how conservatives felt that all this was cheapening the cultural environment. Despite his first-class education, including a law degree from

Harvard, he didn't get any of it. "It's nothing more than a fart on the ocean," he said of the junk polluting the culture. And so, in one smug little sentence, he dismissed the legitimate concerns of tens of millions of ordinary Americans.

Liberals believe that by making "sophisticated" observations like that they're taking a stand against the unwashed masses who want to impose a cultural tyranny on the country. But conservatives don't want the cops to arrest people who produce vile music or cheesy television shows. They don't want the Gestapo to rip up the First Amendment. They're simply concerned about the kind of America we all live in—and how the crap that is washing over our kids every day affects them, and our country. Or as Dan Gerstein, a political operative who used to work for Senator Joe Lieberman, wisely put it: "Most [parents] are just looking for a little cooperation from the captains of culture to make the hard job of raising children in a fully-wired universe a little easier."

Conservatives, I think, understand liberals, mainly because we see their influence everywhere in the culture. They're the ones who make our TV shows and our movies, and who run the music industry. They run our network news divisions and our biggest, most important newspapers. They're the ones who put out our news magazines and our women's magazines. They teach our kids and run our colleges. They're even the comedians on TV, educated smart-asses like Jon Stewart and Stephen Colbert and Bill Maher, who once called George Bush "an emperor—a retarded child emperor." Except for talk radio, liberals pretty much control the culture.

So, much as we might want to, we simply can't avoid them.

Liberals, on the other hand, lead more sheltered lives. Despite what they think, they're far more provincial. If they stay away from just one or two places on the radio or TV dial, they can pretty much escape conservatism in the culture. Which explains why they don't really understand conservatives. Yes, they know some of the bigger names, like Rush Limbaugh and Ann Coulter, but if you live on the Upper West Side of Manhattan or in one of the tonier parts of Los Angeles or in sections of Miami where I live, you've got a better chance of bumping into a redhead from Helsinki than running into a conservative. Which is why my liberal pals can't figure me out.

Frankly, once I made my personal journey to the Dark Side, I was a little surprised myself by what I found. The real, living, breathing conservatives I met were nothing like the caricatures that play in the liberal imagination. By and large, the conservatives I've met in my new incarnation are good, decent folks. They're not bigots, despite what liberals say. And they're certainly not dumb, either. In fact, they're a lot more thoughtful than most of the liberals I used to hang out with. Nuts on the far Right embarrass mainstream conservatives. We cringe when we hear religious leaders blame 9/11 on homosexuals. But I haven't run into a lot of liberals who cringe in the presence of people like Michael Moore, or antiwar icon Cindy Sheehan, who once called President Bush a "lying bastard" and said he was guilty of "war crimes." Conservatives, like everybody else, have their shortcomings, but we're nothing like the evil simpletons that liberals make us out to be.

Conservatism makes more political sense, to me anyway, than liberalism does. Liberals, for example, embrace racial preferences. Supporting affirmative action lets them tell the world, "See, I may be white but I'm not a racist." Conservatives don't understand why a black kid, whose father or mother is a doctor or a lawyer, should get extra points on his college admissions application over a white kid whose father is a cop and whose mother is a waitress. Affirmative action based on financial need is fine as far as we're concerned. But not based on race.

Liberals love open borders. When a liberal sees a few dozen Mexicans coming over the fence in the Southwest, he sees potential

Democratic votes. Conservatives see illegal aliens. We see contempt for our laws, and a bunch of other nasty problems for America—everything from overcrowded public schools to long lines at the hospital for "free" medical care.

Liberals have more faith in the wisdom of government than we conservatives do. Liberals think big government is good, the answer to many of our problems. Conservatives think just the opposite.

The fact is I like conservatism because I'm libertarian on all sorts of issues. If someone needs marijuana to relieve pain from some horrible disease, let him have it, for crying out loud. I part with a lot of conservatives who say there's no proof marijuana provides any medicinal benefits. I say, so what? If someone suffering from cancer even *thinks* it will help, what's the big deal? The world isn't going to come to an end if he smokes a joint.

I take an equally live-and-let-live approach when it comes to gay marriage. I respect the concerns of people of faith. I know all the arguments about where it might lead. But personally, I just don't care if Adam and Steve tie the knot.

I understand that some people believe that life starts at conception. But I simply cannot think of a tiny zygote, no bigger than a period at the end of a sentence, as a person with constitutional rights just like you or me. If it turns out that embryos hold miracles that will cure diseases, then I'm all for using them—and spending tax money for research. I don't see it as "destroying life." I see it as "pro-life."

Basically, I'm the kind of conservative who wants to be left alone. I don't think government does too many things well, so the smaller the government the better I like it. I don't want moralists telling me what to do—not the moralists on the Left, who won't let me eat "unhealthy" foods in restaurants, and not the moralists on the Right, who want to impose their religious beliefs on me and the rest of us who live in a pluralistic society. Which is why

I'm a small-government, let-me-live-my-own-life conservative—like Barry Goldwater, and Ronald Reagan, too.

Which brings me to some unhappy news: The marriage is on the rocks. No, I haven't fallen out of love with *conservatives*. But I'm getting pretty damned tired of those pandering *Republicans*, the ones who got way too comfortable inside the Beltway and who sold out their principles for political power.

These are the ones who tell us they're for small government, and then spend like Democrats. Once, they demonized liberals for spending on every social program under the sun. But when *they* took over, they doled out pork with the best of them—millions for agriculture and highways; millions more for social programs to win over the moderates; add a few trillion for prescription drugs to shore up the senior-citizen vote. Selling your principles doesn't come cheap.

They sold out on immigration, too. A conservative friend got it just right: Bush's immigration policy, he said, is "Don't offend the Hispanics. They might vote Democratic if you do." Hey, we don't want to offend the Hispanics. We want to offend *illegal aliens*! We want to stop the flow of illegals into this country. Then we can talk about "guest-worker programs" and anything else.

The Republicans are no better on race. Liberals—like Thomas B. Edsall, who used to cover politics for the *Washington Post* and who wrote a book called *Building Red America*—believe the Republican Party seeks out white voters "whose interests are overwhelmingly focused on tempering, if not altogether rolling back, the civil rights movement." This is the kind of idiocy Republicans should laugh at. What Republican wants to repeal the Voting Rights Act? Who wants to undo laws that allow blacks to eat at the same lunch counter as whites? Yet, the sheer terror of being tarred with the racist brush has turned many Republicans into sniveling wimps. Once, Republicans like Ronald Reagan were against racial preferences and weren't afraid to say so. Racial preferences put group rights over individual merit. That's not what Republicans stood for. Now, Republicans—taking their cue from the Bush White House—either enthusiastically support affirmative action or head for the hills when the subject comes up.

As for gay marriage: Even if you think it's a bad idea, do we really need a constitutional amendment to ban it? President Bush and Republican leaders in the Senate apparently thought so. They brought it up in Congress. Fortunately, common sense prevailed and the constitutional amendment went nowhere. But respect, nonetheless, was paid to conservative evangelicals, who do vote in big numbers, after all.

I voted for George W. Bush. Twice. I like him. He strikes me as a decent man. But like most conservatives, I know that his "compassionate conservatism" is nothing more than a euphemism for big-government conservatism. And that's not what I signed on for. I'm one of those "small government" conservatives who would like nothing better than for the government to leave me the hell alone.

I'm not comfortable, either, with a party that panders to fundamentalists who think evolution is a fairy tale and figures it's a great idea to teach creationism in science class. I didn't sign on for that, either. Nor did I sign on for nation-building in Iraq. If the war was such a good idea, then we should have had a plan to win it quickly, instead of bleeding slowly.

But please, make no mistake: I'm not going back. By and large, I like it on the Dark Side. I like conservative people and conservative ideas. Am I as enthusiastic with *Republicans* these days? No. But I'm a realist. I understand that some politicians are bad, but others are worse. A conservative friend says too many Democrats seem to think that if we only raise the minimum wage and sign the Kyoto Accords, the terrorists will like us and go away. I know he's half-kidding, but still, I can't be part of anything that even resembles that kind of nonsense anymore. And please understand that nothing I have said here—not a word—is an argument in favor of the mushy middle. Anyone who can't decide between the liberal and the conservative, one week before a presidential election, isn't a moderate. He's a clueless.

The way I see it, Democrats and liberals—again, not all of them, but way too many—have lost their minds. Republicans have lost their nerve. There's a phrase in today's world of sports, which says it all: "Man Up!" That's what they need to do, *Man Up!* A political party either stands for something or it doesn't. Conservatives still believe in important things, but the jury is out on Republicans, the kind who foolishly thought they could hang on to power by betraying their principles. Let's hope Election Day 2006 put an end to that fantasy.

★ ★ ★ ★ ★ ★ ★ ★ ★ ★ ★

Q: Which One Doesn't Belong: George W. Bush, Don Imus, or Charles Barkley?
A: Sir Charles. He's the Only One with the Guts to Tell the Truth About Race

Don Imus and Sir Charles

I got up one morning in January 2006 and turned the TV to MSNBC to watch Don Imus's show, which wasn't always easy. Don can be interesting, and funny, and, of course, needlessly cruel to anyone he doesn't like. But he can also be so boring that your hair begins to hurt. Don, you see, has devoted much of his life to helping sick kids. He's a genuine humanitarian. And for that he deserves our gratitude. But even his own sidekicks wanted to put guns to their heads when he went on and on and on (and on and on) about one of his pet causes—like autism. And when he's not boring the hell out of us with that, he's droning on and on about the nasty chemicals in household window-cleaners and why you should buy the "toxic-free" kind his wife came up with. He also spent a mind-numbing amount of time hawking his salsa and chips, which he sells to raise money for the sick kids.

Sometimes, on a day when the big news was about an earthquake in some third-world country, which left twenty thousand dead, he would whine about how tough it is to be stuck in heavy traffic while sitting in the backseat of his chauffer-driven limousine. If his coffee got cold, he'd act like it was a tragedy on the same scale as the worldwide AIDS epidemic, as one of his own pals once put it. There's no doubt about it: tuning in to *Imus in the Morning* was like watching a freak show hosted by a nasty Mother Teresa in a cowboy hat. He even looks a little like her.

But despite all that, he was still better than a lot of the other banal crap that's on in the morning. (Once, I actually saw a segment on the CBS morning show on how to properly fold sheets.) Imus, on the other hand—when he's not being boring—has an edge. And he went out of his way to convey the impression that he's a tough guy who isn't afraid to say what's on his mind, no matter who might not like it. But in April 2007, when he called the women on the Rutgers basketball team a bunch of "nappy-headed hos"—a dumb, off-the-cuff joke, he insisted—the sensitivity police demanded his head on a platter, which they promptly got. Both NBC, which carried the show on its MSNBC cable network, and CBS, which carried it on radio, fired Imus.

But this was hardly the first time Don Imus made a dumb remark about race. On that January morning in 2006, Imus said something even dopier than his "nappy-headed ho" remark. But this time, he didn't get into *any* trouble. This dumb remark about race didn't even cause of ripple of outrage or concern.

On this particular day he was talking to Charles Barkley, the retired basketball star, whose book about race in America—*Who's Afraid of a Large Black Man?*—had just come out in paperback. They started out by talking about the death, the night before, of Coretta Scott King. Sir Charles, who grew up in Alabama, told Imus how much she and her husband, Martin Luther King Jr., had meant to him.

This gave Don an opening to tell Barkley that, "In my view, just as a white man, it doesn't seem to me that a lot has changed since those marches in Selma."

Just to make sure it sunk in, let me give you that quotation one more time:

"In my view, just as a white man, it doesn't seem to me that a lot has changed since those marches in Selma."

This may be the dumbest single sentence uttered on the subject of race in the twenty-first century, and one of the dumbest ever. The march from Selma to Montgomery was in 1965. Imus was talking to Barkley in 2006. And not much has changed? Has Don been in a coma?

In 1965, blacks were marching in Selma because George Wallace, the segregationist governor, and the other bigots who ran Alabama, wouldn't let them vote. Maybe Imus hadn't noticed, but that changed.

Black people couldn't eat at lunch counters with white people or drink out of the same water fountains. That changed.

Civil rights workers were being murdered and buried in earthen dams. That changed.

White racist sheriffs were turning vicious dogs and water hoses on black people. That changed.

The idea, in those days, that a black man or woman would someday be elected mayor of a town or city in the Deep South was beyond preposterous. That changed, too.

And so did a million other things, big and small.

But, you see, intelligent white people like Don Imus say monumentally dumb things like this mainly because it makes them feel good. He might as well have said, "You see, Charles, I'll say anything, no matter how stupid, just so I can show you my racial sensitivity—because that makes me feel like a decent human being." Actually, more than anything else, it makes the weenies feel *less guilty* about being white.

Don had authors on his show from time to time. Perhaps he should have invited Shelby Steele, a black scholar who wrote a book on the subject, called *White Guilt*. "Whites know on some level," Steele wrote, "that they are stigmatized by their skin color alone, that the black people they meet may suspect them of being racist simply because they are white."

Perhaps Shelby Steele did not have Don Imus specifically in mind when he sat down to write that perceptive sentence, but over the years Steele had met plenty of white people, just like Imus, who said dumb things to show their virtue. "White guilt," Steele says, "does not depend on the goodwill or the genuine decency of people. It depends on their fear of stigmatization, their fear of being called a racist."

This gives us some important insight into why Don Imus could so cavalierly brush away forty years of America's progress and declare that when it comes to race, he hadn't noticed much change in America since 1965. There's always the fear that if you say the "wrong" thing, you'll be seen as a bigot. It's easier simply to say something dumb than run that risk.

But let's give Don Imus the benefit of the doubt. Let's say he isn't as egregiously ignorant as he sounds. Let's say he really knows better but was simply being dishonest to show off his "racial manners." That would put him in some pretty good company.

From the moment our country was founded, dishonesty has been the price of admission to the conversation on race. Remember that line our Founding Fathers came up with and enshrined in the Declaration of Independence? The one about how "All men are created equal." The slaves must have gotten a kick out of that. A century later, we were supposed to believe Americans could really live their lives "separate but equal."

Don Imus's observation—"it doesn't seem to me that a lot has changed since those marches in Selma"—while not as eloquent as "All men are created equal," is just as dishonest.

Except on this particular day, the big black man wasn't buying any of it. When Imus asked Charles Barkley if he agreed that not much had changed since the days of Selma, Sir Charles said, No, he most definitely did not agree. Sounding a lot like Bill Cosby, he told Imus, "We as black people have become our own worst enemy. If you're out there killing other black kids, selling drugs, having kids you can't afford, and not getting your education, you just compound the problem. Racism exists. But there comes a point when you have to say enough is enough."

Imus, as *"just a white man,"* didn't have the guts to say any of that, even though he surely must have known that Barkley was speaking a sad truth. But then Sir Charles—unlike Don Imus and the other sissies who are afraid to talk honestly and openly about race—has both sense and courage, and precious little respect for guilt-ridden white men, or for the niceties of their hollow platitudes about race in America.

So, what we continue to get is timid nonsense from frightened white people consumed by guilt and more than willing to ignore a half century of progress on the matter of race in America; white people who feel most comfortable when they're gingerly tiptoeing around the subject. Too bad important issues like the ones Charles Barkley and Bill Cosby and more than a few black conservatives talk about all the time are too hot for the well-off white weenies to handle. You think they'd show a little more courage if it were their kids who were killing themselves?

In December 2007, some eight months after CBS and NBC fired him, Don Imus was back on the air, this time on WABC radio in New York and other stations around the country. On his first new show, he promised that he would "never say anything in my lifetime that will make any of these young women at Rutgers regret or feel foolish that they accepted my apology and forgave me." Good. But it's too bad Don Imus didn't make another promise while he was at it: to never again be one of those silly white pandering fools who say really dumb things to show their "racial virtue," the way he did with Charles Barkley.

Folding Like a Cheap Accordion—and Other Ways to Pander on Race

Al Sharpton is unhappy. He is complaining to Bill O'Reilly that President Bush finally shows up to speak to the NAACP annual convention in 2006 but during his entire speech doesn't utter so much as a syllable about affirmative action. It's not every day that the Reverend Al and I agree. But we do on this one. Up to a point.

I think the president should have uttered a lot of syllables about affirmative action. And they all should have added up to: "I'm against it!"

He should have told the NAACP delegates that his administration supports programs that help black kids get into college—so long as they're based on merit or on financial need. He should have said he would put the full force of the government to work against racial discrimination wherever it pops up, but that his administration would never back a program that makes skin color a major factor in deciding who gets what.

He should have told the NAACP delegates a whole bunch of things he didn't tell them. And that's the problem with Republicans these days. They've learned to pander with the best of them—meaning, of course, the Democrats.

At least when Democrats pander on racial issues, you get the impression they actually believe what they say. You can't help but be convinced, for example, that the Democrats backed welfare for all those years, no matter how crippling it was to one generation after another of black people, because they really thought it was a good thing. You get the impression that they oppose school vouchers that would let poor black kids escape their crummy public schools, not just because they're in bed with the teachers unions, but also because they really do support the concept of public schools, *in principle*—even while they send their own kids to private schools.

But how can real conservatives favor racial preferences? How can they back an affirmative action program that gives some black kid from a well-to-do suburb of Chicago "bonus admission points" for college at the expense of some blue-collar white kid whose father works in a steel mill in Pennsylvania or West Virginia? Yet, Republicans, by and large, either proudly support racial preferences, or, like President Bush at the NAACP convention, are afraid to even say the words out loud.

It wasn't always this way. Once there were Republicans like Ronald Reagan, who thought affirmative action was the first step to quotas—which meant more, not less, discrimination. "I'm old enough to remember when quotas existed in the U.S. for the purpose of discrimination," he said, "and I don't want to see that happen again." There were always bureaucrats and Democrats to get in the way, but Reagan's position on affirmative action was clear—and it set the tone for the entire Republican Party.

In California, the Republican governor Pete Wilson unapologetically backed Proposition 209, which banned racial preferences in state hiring and college admissions. "It is time for those who have resisted Prop. 209, to acknowledge that equal rights under law, not special preferences, is the law of the land," he said. "A measure that eliminates any form of discrimination based on race and gender violates no one's constitutional rights."

In 1996, Prop 209 passed with 54 percent of the vote. Ward Connerly, the black businessman who led the fight against racial preferences, said that Republican support was "vital." "They provided us with a lot of foot soldiers," he said, "and even more essential, a critical mass of support. Because nobody ever likes to be left standing alone, especially when it comes to race."

So what happened? When did Republicans lose their nerve on race? And why?

I suspect it has something to do with the Democrats' all-purpose bogeyman, Karl Rove, who has always been trolling for votes—even before George W. Bush became a lame duck. Pick up a few black votes here and a few more there, and who knows, maybe it could change the outcome of an election.

But the pandering has its roots not just in political practicality, but also in fear. Race is, after all, the most volatile issue in American life. And for white politicians it's also the most terrifying, "one that, at the merest whiff of a charge of 'racism,' transforms even normally principled leaders into panderers and cowards," as Harry Stein once put it in a piece for *City Journal* magazine.

Ward Connerly says he's seen it happen. "I've often had the experience of speaking in a room of a hundred people, and knowing that ninety-nine of them agree with me," he has said, "but if there's one angry black person in the audience who disagrees, that person controls the room. He'll go on about the last four hundred years, and institutional racism, and 'driving while black,' and the other ninety-nine will just sit there, and fold like a cheap accordion."

★

But let's take a step back for a moment: What was President Bush doing at the NAACP annual convention in 2006 in the first place? This was the first time since he had been elected president that he actually showed up. Every year before that, he refused—and for good reason. After all, this was the group whose chairman, Julian Bond, has said that the Bush administration picked its judicial nominees from "the Taliban wing of American politics" and that the Republican Party wants "to write bigotry back into the Constitution."

This was also the organization that ran a television ad linking then-governor Bush to the brutal murder of James Byrd, a black man who was chained to the back of a pickup truck by three white bigots and dragged along the road until he was dead. Governor Bush had opposed parts of a Texas hate-crime bill, and that was all the NAACP needed to put a white hood over his head.

In 2001, the first year President Bush blew off the NAACP, John McWhorter, the black conservative scholar, endorsed Bush's decision. "If Bush is seriously committed to the Advancement of Colored People," McWhorter wrote, "his first step will be to dissociate himself from this irrelevant shell of an organization. Next year, the president ought to decline the NAACP's annual invitation flat-out and send no videotape as a consolation (as he did this year). Some will seize on this as evidence that Bush is 'anti-black'; but these folks would insist on that regardless, and Bush will just have to chalk them up as losses. Truth be told, there are not nearly as many such people as we are often led to think, and if Bush wants to develop more of a following in black America, he must concentrate on those blacks committed to personal excellence and moving ahead. Sadly—but clearly—that will mean letting the NAACP go its own way."

But at some point along the way, Bush and his administration decided that it would not be wise to let the NAACP go its own way. So here he was, appearing at his first NAACP convention, pandering to an organization whose leadership is still living in the 1960s. This is a group that still believes that its job number one is fighting racial discrimination; that acts as if Bull Connor's cops are still turning their water hoses and German shepherds on black civil rights demonstrators, that black men in Selma are still being beaten by state police during their march to Montgomery, and that the Ku

Klux Klan is still terrorizing black folks late at night on the back roads in Mississippi.

Someone needs to tell the NAACP that America has moved on. The president had the chance, but he just wasn't the man to do it. Reagan might have. Reagan had courage.

"I understand that racism still lingers in America," the president told the NAACP instead that day. "It's a lot easier to change a law than to change a human heart. And I understand that many African-Americans distrust my political party."

Enthusiastic cheers and lots of applause!

"For too long, my party wrote off the African-American vote," the president said, "and many African-Americans wrote off the Republican Party."

More applause.

Had he been brave, Bush could have done what the Democrats rarely do when the subject turns to race. He could have spoken honestly.

The president could have held up a piece by *New York Times* columnist Bob Herbert, who is both liberal and black. "If you don't trust me because I'm white and Republican, then listen to what Bob Herbert has to say," Bush could have said. Then he could have begun reading out loud:

"'One of the cruelest aspects of slavery was the way it wrenched apart black families, separating husbands from wives and children from their parents. It is ironic, to say the least, that now, nearly a century and a half after the Emancipation Proclamation, much of the most devastating damage to black families, and especially black children, is self-inflicted.'"

The biggest problems facing many black people in America these days, Herbert wrote, are linked to behavior and "the corrosion of black family life, especially the absence of fathers."

If Bush had been able to muster the courage to tell the NAACP delegates what they needed to hear, he could have acknowledged that many problems in black America today have their roots in slavery and segregation. But then he could have said that the slave-holders aren't coming back to fix the problem. And neither is any-one else who has wanted to keep blacks in their place. He could have said that government can't stop fifteen-year-old girls from having babies. Nor can it do much to turn absent fathers into real men who will take care of their children. Government can provide free public education, he could have told them, but as a practical matter it can't force kids to pay attention in class and graduate.

He could have told them what Bob Herbert would have told them: That we can all make believe these terrible things aren't really happening but that ignoring the real problems won't help anybody. Nor will it help to put all of the blame on "society" or "govern-ment."

If the president had said anything like that, he might have made a difference. Race is the wound that never seems to heal—mainly because black people in America don't get a lot of straight talk about race, not from white liberal Democrats and not from so-called conservative Republicans, either.

President Bush would have done himself, his party, and, much more important, black America, one great big favor if he had told the convention what Bob Herbert told his *New York Times* read-ers: "I believe that nothing short of a new movement, comparable in scope and dedication to that of the civil rights era, is required to bring about the changes in values and behavior needed to halt the self-destruction that is consuming so many black lives. The crucial question is whether the leadership exists to mount such an effort."

These are the words I would have put in the president's mouth that day: "We will do what we can in government, but you need to lead the way. Forgive me for being blunt," he could have said, "but the NAACP was once a beacon of light, a positive force for change.

It needs to be that again. Either you will meet that challenge or you won't. But let me be honest: The burden is on you a lot more than it's on me or any other politician."

But Bush was unable to muster the courage to speak honestly about race.

When Republicans stoop this low, when they pander like Democrats, when they go before the NAACP but don't have the courage to speak the truth, it's a betrayal of their values—of *our* values.

The president, who envisions a better life for Arabs in the Middle East, can't bring himself to tell the NAACP that he also envisions a better life for black Americans, and for that better life to come to fruition, the black civil rights establishment needs to snap out of it, stop playing the victim card, and start living in the twenty-first century. That would have taken a certain amount of courage, and that is one thing that the Republicans seem to have lost.

And who exactly benefits from this cowardice? Black people? How? Republicans? I don't think so. Anybody?

★ ★ ★ ★ ★ ★ ★ ★ ★ ★ ★

**Q: What's the Difference Between Fox News and Ann Coulter?
A: Ann Coulter Also Drives Some Conservatives Crazy**

Fox Derangement Syndrome

I've been contemplating some very weighty matters of late. Is there a God? What is the meaning of life? Why do liberals hate Fox News?

Let's leave the small stuff to smaller minds and get to what is truly important: Why, indeed, do liberals detest Fox News with such a burning passion? Why do they hate Bill O'Reilly more than Osama bin Laden and almost as much as Dick Cheney? Why, in places like the Upper West Side of Manhattan, do their eyes roll reflexively at the mere mention of the words "Fox News," in much the same way as your leg jerks when the doctor hits your knee with a rubber hammer?

Why, in other words, does Fox News loom so large in the fevered liberal imagination? Why do they see it as a fire-breathing monster with frightening powers aimed at destroying the Democratic Party? Why, especially when you consider that there are 300 million people living in this country and on any given night only about 2 million are watching Fox News, would any rational person think Fox News is the Evil Empire?

The key word, my friends, is "rational." After much study and consideration, I have come to the conclusion that there is nothing even remotely rational about the fear and loathing of Fox News. I have come to the conclusion that liberals who hate Fox are sick. They suffer from a mental disorder that some of us have called . . .

drumroll, please . . . "Fox derangement syndrome" (FDS). Since those who are afflicted with Fox derangement syndrome are irrational, and unable to decipher the root causes of their hatred, let me try to unravel the mystery.

First, more than a few liberals with chronic FDS don't actually watch Fox News. They don't have to. Everyone they know inside the liberal bubble hates Fox News, so, naturally, they hate it, too. I've spoken to people who detest Rush Limbaugh, and when I ask how often they listen to him, they say, "Well . . . never." For many on the Left, it's the same with Fox. Still, there are some tidbits about Fox they have managed to pick up. One is that some evil son of a bitch named Roger Ailes, who used to work for Ronald Reagan, runs the place. Check please! Case closed! What more do they need to know, for crying out loud?

What about Fox's conservative bent—the fact that it's not just one more liberal TV news outfit? Does that make liberals angry? Of course it does—just as the other networks' liberal bent makes conservatives angry. But if you actually watch Fox, you soon discover that they have tons of smart liberals on the air, debating the issues of the day. Tons. There's Susan Estrich, who ran Michael Dukakis's presidential campaign. And Lanny Davis, who used to work for Bill Clinton. There's Eleanor "Rodham" Clift, who works for *Newsweek* and sounds like a flak employed by the Democratic National Party. There's always some left-wing civil liberties lawyer on, complaining about how bad conservatives are. And the Prince of Leftistan, Michael Moore, was even on one night.

All those lefties getting so much face time on Fox should make your run-of-the-mill liberals very happy, right? But it doesn't. Why? Two reasons: First, they don't even notice the liberals on Fox, in much the same way that a fish doesn't notice the water he's swimming in. Seeing liberals on the news seems so natural to liberals that it doesn't register as any big deal. Second, they *do* notice the conservatives who are debating the liberals. They stick out like the proverbial sore thumb. And their very presence—actually, their very existence—makes liberals mad.

This anger leads to a debilitating disorientation. Liberals, remember, are used to getting their news from CBS, PBS, NBC, and ABC. They aren't accustomed to seeing conservatives on television. Can you imagine how they must feel, the poor darlings—the ones who actually watch Fox, that is—when they tune in to *Hannity & Colmes*? They hate Colmes, the liberal, because he isn't crazy enough for them. And they hate Hannity because, well, because he's a conservative. The agony must be unbearable.

And you know what else drives them bonkers? Fox's "Fair and Balanced" slogan. *Oh, how they hate it!* It's like a sharp stick in their eye. How, they scream, can a news operation possibly be "fair and balanced" when it has the gall to present both sides of the argument!

But as much as liberals detest the slogan, there's something—make that some*one*—they detest even more. And that would be the anti-Christ himself. Yes, Bill O'Reilly! True-blue liberals despise him more than everyone else on the network, combined. Yes, Bill can be overbearing and even toplofty. (Look it up, as Bill might say.) But that's not really why they hate him. They hate O'Reilly because he's not one of them. They hate him because he's got lots and lots of fans who love him—*ordinary* Americans who don't live in New York City, who don't hang on every sarcastic word that Frank Rich or Maureen Dowd writes in the *New York Times*, who don't go to incredibly boring foreign films because that's what *so*phisticated people are supposed to do, and who don't think France is a beacon of light in an otherwise dark and dreary world.

But here's a bulletin that liberals somehow managed to miss: Bill O'Reilly is one of the very few anchors on cable TV who have actually uttered the words "That's a good point" to someone they otherwise disagree with. When was the last time one of their heroes, like Michael Moore—or Dan Rather, for that matter (who even in exile is still standing by his Memogate story), said something like that?

But nothing you say about Fox News to someone suffering from FDS ever makes even a tiny dent. Their minds are made up. As far as they're concerned, anyone who has anything to do with Fox, first and foremost, is a moron. This is their great certainty in life, that Fox is a network for boobs, hayseeds, and bigots. But even though this gives libs with Fox derangement syndrome delusions of grandeur, oddly, it doesn't really give them comfort. It just makes them even angrier.

So, in the end, this isn't about Bill O'Reilly, or Sean Hannity, or Brit Hume, or Roger Ailes, or anybody else at Fox. In the end, this is about liberals themselves and the serious psychological problem they're having adapting to a changing world. That's what this is really about—*adapting*! They liked it when the *New York Times* and the other so-called mainstream media had a lock on the news. It made them feel safe and comfortable, like a baby with his blanket. But now that Fox has taken away their blanket, they are understandably confused. And they're throwing a tantrum—just like the one Bill Clinton threw when he went on Fox with Chris Wallace.

To be fair, conservatives didn't like it when, in the days before Fox, the liberal media had no competition. But conservatives know how to deal with stuff like that—mostly because they've always had to. Conservatives had to learn how to live in a liberal-media culture. Liberals never had to adapt to a conservative culture; hence, the confusion, the anger, and ultimately . . . Fox derangement syndrome.

Because this is no laughing matter, I went to a psychologist I know and asked if there's a genuine scientific diagnosis for this condition that has left so many liberal Fox-haters so disoriented. "Yes," she said, "it's called crazy!"

Do the Ends Justify the Meanness?

While I was writing my last book, *100 People Who Are Screwing Up America,* a lot of liberal friends asked if I was going to include Ann Coulter on the list. "No," I would say, "I'm not. I agree with a lot of what she says, and besides, she makes me laugh." But when a conservative friend whose opinions I respect told me I was dead wrong on this one, that Coulter definitely belonged on the list, I started agonizing. Not enough, though. In the end, I left her out.

Then, after *100 People* came out, I did lots of interviews promoting the book, and more than a few times I was asked, "If you're so concerned about civility, why isn't Ann Coulter in your book?" "Yes, Ann says outrageous things," I would concede. "But she says them with a twinkle in her eye."

Some bought it, others didn't. But now, *I'm* not even buying it. Now, Ann has gone too far even for me. Why? Three words: the Jersey Girls.

Let's face it, there's nothing Ann Coulter could do, except maybe get hit by a very big truck, that would make liberals happy. She could wave a magic wand and turn herself into Mary Poppins, and they'd still hate her.

No problem, as far as Ann is concerned. Because however much they hate her, she hates them more. You get the impression that she detests everything—and I mean *everything*—about liberals, that humiliating them is a driving force in her life, and that the angrier they get the happier she is.

I met Ann only once—at a television studio in Manhattan. We got along fine, mostly, as I say, because I usually agree with her and because she makes me laugh, especially when she says things like "Democrats couldn't care less if people in Indiana hate them. But if Europeans curl their lips, liberals can't look at themselves in the mirror." Or "the *New York Times* editorial page is like an Ouija board that has only three answers, no matter what the question. The answers are: higher taxes, more restrictions on political speech, and stricter gun control."

I mean, who can argue with that?

Ann has figured out that in the United States of Entertainment, mere political analysis isn't enough to cut through the clutter. That's not how you become a household name. Being outrageous is the way to the top these days. Of course, being tall and blond and wearing slinky black dresses helps, too.

But being Ann Coulter isn't as easy as it looks. You have to keep upping the ante just to maintain your status as the blond provocateur. So she has suggested that "a baseball bat is the most effective way" to deal with liberals, that Democrats are "gutless traitors," that "we need somebody to put rat poison in Justice Stevens's crème brûlée," that we should invade countries that hide Muslim terrorists, "kill their leaders, and convert them to Christianity," and she's even lamented that Oklahoma City bomber Timothy McVeigh "did not go to the *New York Times* building."

I think she's kidding, but I wouldn't bet on it.

One way or the other, this is red meat for red-state America. After all, everyone understands that you have to take sides in a culture war. Criticizing someone on your team is against the rules, tantamount to giving ammunition to the enemy, no matter how much she might deserve it. Liberals support the likes of Michael

Moore and Al Franken, conservatives say, so why shouldn't they support their very own bomb-thrower?

In a culture where the lines are sharply drawn and passions run high, this may be understandable. But it's also a mistake. One that hurts Ann's team more than it hurts liberals.

Going after the *New York Times* is one thing, but going after women whose husbands were killed on September 11, 2001—*the way she did*—is something else altogether, even if they were outspoken political activists who endorsed John Kerry for president. In her book, *Godless, the Church of Liberalism*, Ann put the four "Jersey Girls" in her crosshairs and wrote, "These broads are millionaires, lionized on TV and in articles about them, reveling in their status as celebrities and stalked by griefparrazies. I have never seen people enjoying their husbands' death so much."

And "how do we know," Ann asked, that "their husbands weren't planning to divorce these harpies?" And then one more shot to the solar plexus for good measure: "Now that their shelf life is dwindling, they'd better hurry up and appear in *Playboy*."

Yes, Ann Coulter knows how to operate in the marketplace. She knows how to work the crowd. She understands that as long as she's willing to toss a few grenades she'll get on the *Today* show and everyplace else. She knows this will catapult her book straight to number one on the bestseller lists and will ensure another multimillion-dollar advance for her next book. In other words, Ann understands that *Ann* is the message.

The best I can figure, Ann not only doesn't care what liberals think—she doesn't care what conservatives think, either. She doesn't care what *anybody* thinks. The problem is that she gives liberals a great big club to bang over the heads of conservatives. She gives liberals, who don't need any excuse to hate conservatives, the golden opportunity to say, "See, that's how they *all* are."

Which is why a lot of conservatives have begun speaking out

against Ann. Ed Morrissey, who runs the Captain's Quarters blog, said Coulter had "lost her humanity." Hugh Hewitt, the radio talk-show host, said Coulter owes the widows an apology. Even her friend Bill O'Reilly said, "Once you get down to that level, you often lose the point."

Exactly. Coulter was complaining that Democratic messengers—like the New Jersey widows and Cindy Sheehan, whose son was killed in Iraq—are virtually bulletproof; that they get a free pass no matter how political they are, simply because of their status as grieving widows and mothers. Coulter was saying, screw that! If you enter the political fray, if you take sides, then you open yourself up to criticism—even if your husband was killed on 9/11 or your son was killed in a war. And on this, Ann Coulter is absolutely right.

She's also right about the central point of her book: that liberals who have nothing but contempt for religion, who think fundamentalists are scary, nonetheless have created a religion of their own—a godless, secular one called Liberalism—whose followers (even if they don't see it) are just as orthodox and devout about *their* religion as the people they despise are about theirs.

But the validity of Ann's arguments has been lost in the war of words over the "harpies" who are "enjoying their husbands' death so much." It's too bad Ann couldn't bring herself to simply make the important points without the fireworks. "But that's just not the way she earns a living," as my pal Michael Smerconish, another conservative radio talk-show host and newspaper columnist put it.

No, that's not the way she earns a living. Ann Coulter understands our culture better than almost anyone. She understands that what you say is important, but in the United States of Entertainment, how you say it is even more important. Ann understands that it pays to be *the* blond who throws bombs at liberals. In fact, she understands that it pays very well.

★ ★ ★ ★ ★ ★ ★ ★ ★ ★ ★

Just What We Need: A City with Rice-A-Roni *and* a Foreign Policy . . . and Four Other Reasons Liberals Are Even Crazier Than We Thought

Was I in a Coma When San Francisco Seceded?

I used to live in San Francisco, back in the late '70s. I was a correspondent with CBS News at the time and did my share of goofy stories about the city that we used to call Halloween-by-the-Sea. But even when I took a shot at some of the strange people who lived there—the woman who left her substantial estate to her dog comes to mind—it was always in a good-natured, fun kind of way—mainly because I liked San Francisco. I liked the fact that it was easygoing and tolerant. Tolerance, in fact, is precisely what made San Francisco the liberal city that it was.

No more.

The meaning of the word *liberal* has changed a lot over the past twenty-five years, and so has San Francisco. Too many liberals have forgotten how to be liberal. Too many live in a state of perpetual anger. Read the left-wing blogs some time if you want to see sheer, unadulterated hate up close and personal. But most of all, too many liberals these days think America is the number-one bully in the world, an indication, I'm afraid, of just how bankrupt their liberalism has become. In some strange way, it makes them feel good to think of their own country as a cruel superpower bent on world domination. And this is where San Francisco fits into the picture.

San Francisco liberals still throw the word *tolerant* around just as they always have. But they don't seem to understand the concept anymore—especially when the United States military is involved.

It's no bulletin that a lot of people in San Francisco have opposed the war in Iraq from day one. In fact, a few years back, America's role in the war was put to a citywide vote in a resolution that read: "Shall it be City policy to urge the United States government to withdraw all troops from Iraq and bring all military personnel in Iraq back to the United States?" The get-out-of-Iraq side won in a landslide—63 percent to 37 percent.

Great.

Just what this country needs: a city with Rice-A-Roni *and* a foreign policy.

But one feel-good vote for show wasn't nearly enough to satisfy the crazy Left in San Francisco.

In another election, San Franciscans voted—60 percent to 40 percent—to ban military recruiters from their public schools. Funny, I thought liberals were the ones who were always telling us that "choice" is a good thing. I guess that only applies to abortions; not to choosing whether or not you want to let students listen to a military recruiter talk about a career with the army, navy, air force, or marines. And even though the vote is "only" symbolic—officially, it's nonbinding—it does tell us how these people feel about being citizens of the United States of America.

The city's Board of Supervisors—whose votes *are* binding—doesn't seem to like the military very much, either. After the Bay Area's congressional delegation secured $3 million to bring the USS *Iowa* to San Francisco—to serve as a floating museum—the supervisors voted 8 to 3 against it. They didn't want the World War II/Korean War–era ship anywhere near the Port of San Francisco, even though a study had shown it would bring in half a million visitors a year.

The reason they gave for voting against the museum was their opposition to the war in Iraq and the military's "don't ask don't tell" policy regarding gays. But we all know those aren't the real reasons they voted against the museum. As one San Francisco journalist, Cinnamon Stillwell, put it, "These issues are simply being used as excuses to cover up anti-military and anti-American sympathies across the board."

And that's the real problem. Not whether they want a ship docked in their harbor. Or whether they want kids to go into some safer line of work than the military. It's not even the fact that what they really want is to turn San Francisco into a "military-free zone." It's about something much bigger. It's about their utter *contempt* for the military and even more important, their utter contempt for the rest of America.

San Francisco liberals not only think America is a country that shoots first and asks questions later (at least when a Republican is in the White House), you get the impression they don't think much of Americans, either, specifically the ones who live east of their city and west of Manhattan. They see "ordinary" Americans as unpolished, not nearly as sophisticated as they are. In a word, San Francisco liberals are French! And if they ever get attacked out there in their military-free zone, that's who they should call for help—the French!

After the vote to keep the USS *Iowa* out of San Francisco, City Supervisor Chris Daly said, "I am sad to say I am not proud of the history of the United States of America since the 1940s." Wow! I guess the progress we've made in civil rights and women's rights and yes, gay rights, too, doesn't count. When you have contempt for America, you say such things—and you become a hero to the crazies on the Left.

Even New York, a city with more than its fair share of left-wingers, won't go as far as San Francisco. For about twenty-five years, the USS *Intrepid*, which first saw action in World War II, has been anchored peacefully as a military museum on the Hudson River right there in midtown Manhattan—a tribute to America's historic fight against tyranny. But San Francisco won't even tolerate that much. That's what happens when an entire metropolis is taken over by these kinds of liberals—and decent, sensible people become the ones on the fringe.

Then in 2006, just when you thought they had shown all the contempt they possibly could, the left-wing crazies in San Francisco did it again. This time the school board voted to throw Junior ROTC programs out of the city's high schools, despite the fact that the programs were optional and immensely popular with the kids who chose to join. There was no "don't ask don't tell" issue, either. Anyone could join, and more than a few gay students did. Still, one school board member said it was better to focus on a "curriculum of peace" than allow JROTC to remain as an after-school activity. If any other American city hates the military as much as San Francisco does, I don't know which one it is.

When I lived in San Francisco, Dianne Feinstein, now a United States senator, was mayor of the city. All of this has gotten her down. Regarding the vote to keep the USS *Iowa* out, she told the *San Francisco Chronicle*, "This isn't the San Francisco that I've known and loved and grew up in and was born in. I thought that in view of what's going on and in view of the loss of lives of our men and women, it was a very petty decision."

Dianne Feinstein is a loyal Democrat; she's a liberal the way liberals used to be—before the crazies hijacked the movement.

Alec Baldwin Is Not
Saddam Hussein—
at Least I Don't Think So

Alec Baldwin is angry. Not at President Bush or at any of the other usual conservative suspects. This time he's mad at his ex-wife, the beautiful actress Kim Basinger.

In an interview with *GQ* in October 2006, Baldwin talks about how ugly their divorce got and about how there were days when things got so bad that "I wanted to die on the spot. . . . I would say, 'Please don't let me wake up. I can't face another day.'"

"My ex-wife once said, 'He's Saddam Hussein.' She said that," Baldwin told *GQ*. "And I thought, 'Do I hide myself in cramped underground quarters? Do I like to shoot firearms in a celebratory way? Did I execute whole villages of people and bulldoze their bodies into a pit? What are you saying? Explain this to me?'"

Alec Baldwin has every right to be mad. He may be a lot of things—hotheaded liberal bigmouth comes to mind—but I'm pretty sure he's no mass murderer. And comparing him to one is a smear that should not be tolerated, not even in Hollywood, where nastiness has a certain cachet. So, good for Alec Baldwin!

Now, Alec, stand up and go public again, and this time tell your liberal Hollywood pals that just as you're not Saddam, Bush isn't Hitler. Forgive the unsolicited advice, but here's what you might want to say:

"Does Bush issue orders requiring that certain groups, like Jews and gays, wear badges and ribbons marking them as undesirables targeted for extermination? Does he force his enemies into gas chambers? Did he ever map out a master plan to annihilate an entire people?"

After they stutter for several minutes, Baldwin can tell them that while he understands their childlike need for instant gratification, while he knows how good they feel as soon as the words "Bush is a Nazi" cascade over their surgically enhanced lips, they must learn to control themselves; that words really do have meanings, and by throwing them around so recklessly all they're doing is cheapening what's left of political discourse in America.

Their first reaction, of course, will be "Huh?" But then Alec can explain it to them again—and again and again and again, if necessary—until they get it.

And Alec Baldwin is just the guy to do it. He's got the chops. The presence. And he's a lot smarter than most people in his line of work. I'm not saying he can single-handedly put an end to the ugliness that emanates from the beautiful people, but I think he, of all people out there, might be able to get them to tone down the rhetoric.

Still, that would only solve part of the problem. Unfortunately, it's not simply that words have lost their meaning in our superheated political culture. It's also that a lot of what the entertainment geniuses say just isn't very smart.

Take Rosie O'Donnell. On *The View*, she said that "Radical Christianity is just as threatening as radical Islam in a country like America." Despite the fact that this is really, really stupid, a bunch of starry-eyed Rosie fans in the audience applauded enthusiastically. Does it not occur to Rosie, or her fans, that not even the most "radical" Christians—which I guess is supposed to mean the Republican Born-again type—fly airplanes into buildings? Or commit mayhem because a cartoon has offended them? Or talk about killing the pope because he said something they don't like?

No, Rosie, "radical Christianity" is not just as threatening as radical Islam. Not even close. You may not agree with the politics of fundamentalist Christians on gay marriage or a number of other things, but to compare them to terrorists is shameful and, as I say, not very smart.

A few months later, Rosie pulled off the impossible. She outdid herself in the dumb department. This time she said, again on *The View*, that we Americans should not "fear the terrorists." Why not? Because—and these are her exact idiotic words—"they're mothers and fathers." So were a lot of the Nazis, Rosie!

Once upon a time, Rosie O'Donnell was the "Queen of Nice." These days, she's the "Queen of Stupid," ruling over a land of morons who hang on her every word and actually think she's profound. And she gets to spout off, five days a week, on a television show that is broadcast not just in New York City, where her dumb observations might be considered intelligent, but on ABC, a mainstream national television network. You think ABC (or NBC or CBS) would ever give Ann Coulter such a forum to mouth off against liberals? Sorry I asked.

If this level of stupidity were only confined to entertainers, perhaps we could laugh it off. But no such luck. These days the silliness infects even supposedly serious newspeople. In 2007, a journalist named Chris Hedges came out with a book charmingly, if not subtly, entitled, *American Fascists: The Christian Right and the War on America*. In it, we get a dose of the usual left-of-center moral equivalence. "The Christian Right and radical Islamists," Hedges writes, "although locked in a holy war, increasingly mirror each other." Inane? Of course! But what caught my attention wasn't simply that Hedges comes off as shrill or that he appears to be as shallow as Rosie O'Donnell, troubling as that may be. What I find so interesting is that this view of American life isn't coming from some far-out leftist whom we might easily dismiss. Chris Hedges spent fifteen years working—where else?—at the *New York Times*, where he even won a Pulitzer! No, the crazies to the left of me aren't a bunch of radical nuts who drool on themselves and embarrass ordinary liberals. They *are* ordinary liberals. They're part of the very fabric of *mainstream* liberalism!

Another supposedly serious journalist whose comments indicate otherwise is Bob Schieffer, the CBS News correspondent, former anchorman, and host of *Face the Nation*. Schieffer went on the *CBS Evening News with Katie Couric* and delivered a commentary about how President Bush, by establishing secret prisons overseas to interrogate terrorists, was "adopting the tactics of our enemies."

This is the famous if-we-do-such-and-such-then-we're-no-better-than-they-are argument, and it's as shallow as Rosie O'Donnell's crack about Christians and terrorists. "Democracies have no business running secret prisons," Schieffer said. "That's what our enemies do."

Not really, Bob. When terrorists capture American soldiers, they don't imprison them. Not for long, anyway. They mutilate them, behead them, burn them, and toss their bodies on the side of the road to rot. And if there's a camera around, they tape the whole thing and broadcast it on Al Jazeera.

"If we are in a battle for the hearts and minds of people around the world, as the administration says we are," Schieffer said, "I won't feel very secure if the people around the world believe we are no different than our enemies."

If people around the world think we're no different than our enemies, then these are people who should not be taken seriously. And besides, when I start worrying about what the French and other Western European wimps think, please shoot me! Anyone who equates us with terrorists lacks moral standing to take part in the conversation. And that would include my former colleague Bob Schieffer, who concluded his commentary with this brilliant observation: "We gain nothing by adopting the methods of our enemies."

We don't gain much, either, by listening to this drivel.

Or to Senator John McCain's nonsense about how we run the risk of becoming just like the bad guys. On September 20, 2006, McCain told Don Imus on his morning radio and TV show, "What's so interesting about this argument is that, 'Well, they cut off people's heads so it's okay for us to cut off people's heads.' That's not what America is supposed to be all about." *Who ever said it was? And who—other than some drunk in a bar—has ever said we should cut off their heads because they cut off our heads?* This is the flimsiest of straw men. It says: "You see, I'm on the moral high ground. I care about American values more than you do." Except the whole argument is built on a fairy tale. A made-up quote. It's just more drivel.

Despite all the hand-wringing that we're in danger of becoming *them*, it's not going to happen. The simple fact is that we are better than they are. So-called radical Christians are not the same as radical Muslims. Islam—in the hands of extremists—is a religion of perpetual grievance. Terrorists are, in the eloquent words of Dan Henninger of the *Wall Street Journal*, "history's latest homicidal utopians." We are not. And establishing secret prisons does not put us in the same moral sewer that the terrorists inhabit. Even if the CIA "aggressively" interrogates terrorists, that's not the same as cutting their heads off and mutilating their corpses. What we do is a far cry from "adopting the methods of our enemies." The other side is dedicated to killing as many innocent people as they can. We're not. Most Americans understand that.

All of this reminds me of those folks you see from time to time on the side of the road with posters saying war is bad. They mean well, but these are not serious people. Anyone who might have said anything like that during World War II would have been dismissed as a fool—by liberals and conservatives alike! Back then Americans from both parties understood the dark nature of our enemy. No one in his right mind, back then, would have compared FDR to Hitler or slander fundamentalist Christians by equating them with Nazis. And I'm pretty sure Alec Baldwin would have slapped somebody silly if he did.

John Wayne, Girly Men, and the Democratic Party

So I'm listening to Rush Limbaugh, and this guy named Bill comes on and says he's had it with SNAGs.

Rush has the same question I do: What exactly is a SNAG? A SNAG, Bill informs us, is an acronym for Sensitive New-Age Geek. "You know, the kind of men who end sentences with an upward inflection." This, the very perceptive Bill explains to us, "indicates uncertainty and insecurity."

Bill is definitely on to something very important, especially for the Democratic Party. Because, even though I haven't commissioned a Gallup poll, I'm pretty sure that SNAGs are just about the only straight white men in America who still vote for Democrats in presidential elections. In many ways they represent the backbone (excuse the expression) of today's Democratic Party, which is why all those other white guys abandoned the Democrats a long time ago.

Yes, I know, in the 2006 midterm elections men voted for Democrats in bigger numbers than usual. But trust me, this does not represent a trend. When Republicans find the principles they lost while they were busy getting too comfortable in Washington, when they stop acting like wimps, all those non-SNAG men will return to the fold. But just in case they need a little encouragement, I'm sure the mere sight of those HILLARY CLINTON FOR PRESIDENT bumper stickers will provide it.

SNAGs fret more than most men. They spend a lot of time being afraid. They're afraid, for example, that a Republican president who would listen in on terrorist phone calls without a warrant will also listen in on their phone calls.

SNAGs worry that we're too mean to terrorists and lock them up in bad places.

SNAGs worry, despite tons of evidence to the contrary, that we still live in a racist country.

SNAGs are downright despondent over global warming, convinced that some time between now and next Tuesday icebergs will melt and drown them as they eat stuff I can't pronounce, in their impossibly cute overpriced bistros whose names I can't pronounce, either.

SNAGs worry about how they look in those cashmere sweaters they tie around their necks.

In other words, SNAGs are Girly Men.

Real Men say, "Kill every last one of those bastard terrorists, and I don't care how you do it." Real Men vote for Republicans.

Which brings us to John Wayne, the quintessential Republican. A Harris poll informs us that the Duke is a favorite of conservatives. Who do liberals like? Johnny Depp.

Let's see if I have this right: John Wayne storms the beach at Iwo Jima, puts a bullet in every bad guy in sight, and makes no apologies, because they started it. Johnny Depp dresses up like a pirate and wears eyeliner. I rest my case!

When men of a certain age fantasize about kicking somebody's ass, they see themselves as John Wayne, not Johnny Depp. Try to think of one potential Democratic candidate who reminds you of John Wayne. Joe Biden? Dennis Kucinich? John Edwards? Hillary? Which of them appeals to white men? Exactly. None of them! They don't even appeal to married women who, might I add, are no big fans of SNAGs or other Democrats, either. In the 2004 presidential election married women went 55 percent to 44 percent for W.

But Republicans are always posing like the Duke. There was Reagan, who looked great in a cowboy hat; and Bush, who's always being called a cowboy. McCain comes from cowboy country and can ride a horse. My God, even Rudy Giuliani, who was born in Brooklyn, resembles John Wayne more than any Democrat does.

★

By some strange alignment of the planets, on the very same day I was learning about SNAGs, the syndicated columnist Richard Cohen had a piece in my local newspaper, the *Miami Herald*, about the Duke. Cohen nailed the Democrats' dilemma in one brilliant sentence: "The one thing [John Wayne] and the Democratic Party have in common is that they are both dead."

The Democrats came back to life in 2006. But if it's Hillary vs. Rudy or McCain or even Mitt Romney in '08, the SNAG vote won't be enough to save her.

We're All Doomed. Or Not

I'm talking to my liberal friend Gary, and because it's been in the news so much, I bring up the subject of global warming.

"I'm not convinced the threat is real," I tell him.

In a very calm and gentle tone one might use when speaking to a moron, he asks me, "Are you convinced that gravity is real?"

That was a nice way, I guess, of saying, *"You're a crackpot!"* But why? I didn't say the Earth is flat. I didn't say Mickey Mantle assassinated JFK. I simply said I'm not sure that global warming is as bad as a lot of people seem to think. I might as well have told him I thought the Holocaust was a fairy tale.

You see, as far as many (mostly liberals) are concerned, global warming is an absolute fact—as real as the Holocaust. Which, I guess, explains why CBS News correspondent Scott Pelley, who had just done a gloom-and-doom global-warming piece for *60 Minutes*, told an interviewer who asked him why his story was so one-sided: "If I do an interview with [Holocaust survivor] Elie Wiesel, am I required as a journalist to find a Holocaust denier?"

The question was rhetorical, of course. Pelley, and about a gazillion other so-called mainstream journalists, obviously think the case is closed on global warming: It's real and anyone who doesn't think so is ignorant. Which is why he also said, "There comes a point in journalism where striving for balance becomes irresponsible."

Balance, you see, is for *controversial* stories. And since there's nothing controversial about global warming, why be "irresponsible" and "strive for balance"? Would any reporter in his right mind try to find someone to say the sun comes up in the *west*, just because everyone with a brain says it comes up in the *east*?

The problem with this reasoning—a term I'm using loosely—is that the sun *does* come up in the east. Finding some idiot who says it doesn't would indeed be irresponsible. The Holocaust *did* happen, no matter how many fools say it didn't. But should we put global warming in the same category?

Well, there certainly is enough circumstantial evidence on global warming for reasonable people to be concerned. So my gripe isn't so much with global warming as it is with liberals—one of whose many problems is that they live in an echo chamber. And when it comes to global warming, all they're getting in there is one side of the story. Which is precisely why they think there only *is* one side of the story.

This brings us to someone most liberals have never heard of, since he wrote about global warming not on the op-ed page of the *New York Times* but on the op-ed page of the *Wall Street Journal*. His name is Richard Lindzen, and he happens to be a professor of atmospheric science at MIT. In a piece titled "There Is No 'Consensus' on Global Warming," he wrote, "According to Al Gore's new film 'An Inconvenient Truth,' we're in for 'a planetary emergency': melting ice sheets, huge increases in sea levels, more and stronger hurricanes and invasions of tropical disease, among other cataclysms—unless we change the way we live now."

This, Professor Lindzen said, was nothing more than "shrill alarmism." To believe *An Inconvenient Truth*, he said, required ignoring a few inconvenient facts. Such as:

★ The Arctic was warm or warmer in the 1940s than it is today

★ Alpine glaciers have both retreated *and* advanced over the years

★ They have been retreating since the early nineteenth century; but were advancing for seven centuries before that

★ Since about 1970, many of the glaciers have stopped retreating and some are now advancing again ("And frankly," Professor Lindzen asserts, "we don't know why.")

★ Hurricane frequency and strength have varied over long periods of time

★ The temperature of the ocean surface—which affects hurricanes—also varies over long periods of time

★ The general global temperature itself has gotten both warmer and cooler over time

★ Malaria, which liberals claim is a by-product of global warming, is common in Siberia, a place not exactly known for its heat

In other words, it's not such a conclusive certainty, after all (no matter what Al Gore and the mainstream media say), that thanks to man's unconscionable recklessness—and make no mistake, *that's* why they hate global warming so much—we're all perched on the brink of destruction. But what if global warming isn't *man's* doing after all? What if it's just a *natural* cycle we're currently in. Oh, how that would upset liberals, who aren't happy unless they're blaming money-grubbing (conservative) polluters or other *ecologically insensitive cretins* for destroying the planet.

As for Mr. Doomsday: "A general characteristic of Mr. Gore's approach," the professor says, "is to assiduously ignore the fact that the earth and its climate are dynamic; they are always changing even without any external forcing. To treat all change as something to fear is bad enough; to do so in order to exploit that fear is much worse."

I don't want to give anyone the wrong impression. I care about global warming as much as the next guy. Okay, that's not entirely true; especially if the next guy is Al Gore or Scott Pelley. But I really do care. Who wants more hurricanes? Not me; I live in Miami. And no one wants famine and disease.

But here's the rub: I keep thinking I'm going to wake up one day and the same mainstream media that are bombarding me with global-warming stories are going to start hitting me over the head with stories about how we're all about to freeze to death. And I've got good reason to be suspicious. It's happened before.

Thanks to some meticulous research by a conservative media-watchdog group called the Business & Media Institute (BMI), I have learned that in 1924, the *New York Times* ran stories about "A New Ice Age." Then, in 1933, the paper reported on "The Longest Warming Spell Since 1776." And then in 1975, the *Times*, like the weather, changed again, this time writing about "A Major Cooling Widely Considered to Be Inevitable." Now, as we all know, it's back to the global warming.

The Business & Media Institute went even further back into the archives and discovered that the media has been bouncing between hot and cold for more than a hundred years. Back in the late 1800s they were running stories about the dangers of global cooling. As the *New York Times* put it in a headline on February 24, 1895, "Geologists Think the World May Be Frozen Up Again."

But the *New York Times* isn't the only publication sending mixed messages. In 1923, *Time* magazine was also worried about global cooling. "The discovery of changes in the sun's heat and the southward advance of the glaciers in recent years," *Time* confidently reported, "have given rise to conjectures of the possible advent of a new ice age." But in 1939, *Time* told its readers that "Weather men have no doubt that the world at least for the time being is growing warmer." Then in 1974, *Time* was back to pushing the dangers of global cooling. Experts, *Time* said, "are becoming increasingly apprehensive, for the weather aberrations they are studying may be the harbinger of another ice age." And by 2001, *Time* was telling its readers that "scientists no longer doubt that global warming is happening."

Anyone else confused?

The problem seems obvious: As smart and as sophisticated as these scientists may be, they don't seem to understand that we're just a dot in history; that fifty years from now other modern, sophisticated, and intelligent scientists may very well state (again, with absolute certainty) that if we don't change our ways, global catastrophe will surely follow—as we all turn into frozen Popsicles.

From all of this back-and-forth, I have come to two basic conclusions: First, at any given time, scientists don't know nearly as much as they think they do. And second, journalists know even less. They may often be wrong, these fearless liberal reporters, but they are rarely in doubt. Once they ran doomsday stories about cataclysmic catastrophes that would surely be brought on by global cooling. Now they run stories about cataclysmic catastrophes that will just as surely be brought on by global warming.

★

On January 14, 2007, the *New York Times* took its coverage of the global-warming crisis to a whole new level. On that day the newspaper of record revealed how calamitous the global-warming problem is *right now*, especially in places like New York City. The new information appeared in a column by Jonathan Miles entitled "Saving the Toddy"—a groundbreaking piece of journalism on the life and death struggles of polar bears in the Arctic and hot toddies in Manhattan.

Yes, you read that right!

The column begins: "By proposing to add polar bears to the list of 'threatened species' last month, the Bush administration seemed to finally acknowledge that global warming is taking a toll. . . . Closer to home and heart, I'd been worrying about another sort of species that . . . seems terribly vulnerable to climate change: the hot toddy."

You can't make this stuff up!

Here's the problem according to the *Times*: "Like polar bears, these cold-weather cocktails depend upon frigid temperatures to survive. And frigid temperatures have been a conspicuous no-show in New York this winter." What to do? "As with wildlife species," the *Times* writes, "the key to survival may be adaptability."

And just how do you adapt? Well, instead of imbibing hot toddies when the weather is balmy in the middle of winter, the *Times* says you might want to consider downing a few *cold* toddies!

And there you have it: The most important newspaper in the history of the world ingeniously managed to drag global warming, threatened polar bears, and George W. Bush bashing into a single story about how to turn a hot toddy into a cold toddy in order to save an alcoholic beverage from extinction!

And my liberal friend Gary thinks *I'm* the crackpot?

So-called
Apocalypse
Now

Why do you think liberals never use the term
"*so-called* global warming" but are always referring to the "*so-called* war on terror"? Is it because they fear a one-degree change in temperature *over the next hundred years* more than they fear being blown up by a terrorist *next week*? Is it because they think global warming is *real* and the war on terror is *fake*?

Well, in a word, yes. The fact is a lot of liberals think the war on terror is nothing more than a cynical Republican scare tactic carefully designed to trample all over our civil liberties. But liberals' skepticism goes beyond that.

For a lot of liberals, it's personal. They simply hate George W. Bush. And that colors everything. If Bush says up, they say down. If he says white, they feel compelled to say black. And if he calls it "the war on terror," they have to call it "the so-called war on terror." They simply cannot help themselves. In fact, I'm pretty sure that if, in his inauguration speech, President Bush had said, "We must unite to combat global warming," liberals would have, from that moment on, referred to it as "so-called global warming."

Why do liberals hate Bush so much? It can't just be because of his politics. You think they'd suddenly love him if he signed the Kyoto Accords? Not a chance! It can't be because he said there were weapons of mass destruction in Iraq. Everyone, including a whole gaggle of liberal Democrats, said the exact same thing. They can't hate him, either, because he's against abortion. A lot of people are against abortion. So why do they detest him so much?

Because George W. Bush stands for a whole constellation of values and beliefs they grew up loathing: He's unapologetically religious; he wears his patriotism on his sleeve (and on his lapel); he thinks America is not only a good and moral nation, but better than anything they've got over there in Western Europe. They hate him because he doesn't read the books they read or watch the television shows they watch; they hate him because he's from Texas; and, of course, they hate his bad grammar, which the elites see as something akin to a character flaw or a birth defect. In other words, they hate him because they think he's stupid! I am constantly amused by how such a "dumb" and "simple" guy as George W. Bush can drive so many "sophisticated" liberals around the bend.

This unfortunate condition that afflicts so many on the Left actually has a name. It's called Bush derangement syndrome (BDS), so designated by the Pulitzer Prize–winning columnist Charles Krauthammer, who, might I add, trained at Harvard to be a psychiatrist (he knows derangement when he sees it!). BDS, according to Krauthammer, is "the acute onset of paranoia in otherwise normal people in reaction to the policies, the presidency—nay—the very existence of George W. Bush."

BDS should not be confused with FDS, Fox derangement syndrome, although the two do have an awful lot in common.

You see BDS in all sorts of liberal places. Take the "letters to the editor" section of the *New York Times*. A man from California writes: "The so-called war on terror has provided political cover for a raw assertion of unchecked executive power." Translation: Bush came up with the "so-called" war on terror not to fight terrorists, but to take every last one of our civil liberties away so he could personally read our mail and listen in on our phone calls—that is, when he's not watching reruns of *Hee Haw*.

Another scary thing about Bush derangement syndrome is that you don't even have to be American to have it. Nobel Prize–winning Egyptian author Naguib Mahfouz calls "the so-called war on terrorism . . . just as despicable a crime" as the September 11 attack on the United States. A left-wing politician in London writes in the *Guardian* newspaper about the "so-called" war on terror in a piece that runs under the headline "This War on Terrorism Is Bogus: The 9/11 Attacks Gave the US an Ideal Pretext to Use Force to Secure its Global Domination."

How does a psychological disorder like BDS become such a worldwide epidemic? Ever hear of CNN? On its Web site, CNN ran a picture with this caption: "U.S. President George W. Bush gains reassurances from Pakistani President Pervez Musharraf that Pakistan is doing everything it can to help in the so-called war on terror."

Sometimes the war on terror goes by another name: World War III. But don't ever say those words anywhere near anyone with Bush derangement syndrome. It drives them even nuttier. Case in point: I was listening to Air America one day (no kidding!) and I heard a host and her producer howling over the fact that conservatives often refer to the war on terror as World War III. They put together a montage of conservative voices saying the words "World War III" over and over and over again. When the tape finally ended they laughed it up and talked about what a bunch of jerks these right-wingers were.

★

Sorry. I don't get the joke. Whether they actually call it World War III or not, most Americans take the threat from radical, violent Muslims pretty seriously. I understand that it's not a bulletin that Air America is out of sync with Real America, but what exactly did these two find so funny?

Part of it, I guess, is that the Air America folks—and plenty of other liberals, too—don't really think we're involved in a war against Muslim terrorists, a global war with the free world on one side and the modern-day fascists on the other. They think that "World War III" is just a Republican talking point; that all the conservative stooges who go on the Fox News channel and talk about World War III are part of a vast right-wing conspiracy to help George W. Bush turn America into Nazi Germany and kill innocent civilians in misbegotten foreign wars. And, oh yeah, they yuck it up about World War III because *they're nuts*!

But you also see Bush derangement syndrome in more respectable places than Air America, like, say, the Mecca of liberal sensibilities, the op-ed page of the *New York Times*—which twice a week runs columns by Paul Krugman. Go to Bush derangement syndrome in the *Diagnostic and Statistical Manual of Mental Disorders* and you will see a picture of Mr. Krugman.

But I have another sufferer of Bush derangement syndrome in mind at the moment: Sarah Vowell, the author and regular on NPR, whom the *Times* took on as a guest columnist for a while in 2006 to fill in for regulars who were off causing trouble elsewhere. One of her columns in particular caught my eye. It was about a reading she had done in a bookstore on the West Coast, "where at least five people will hiss like snakes and radiators if an author even mentions the names of certain senior administration officials." (Only five? Are the others deaf or something?)

Ms. Vowell said that during the Q & A session that followed, a man asked her to give him a reason to be optimistic. The question, she tells us, threw her, because "My go-to worldview is pessimism."

Ms. Vowell tells us she was taken aback by the request for optimism, so she "mumbled something about seeking solace in art and the land." But even as she uttered those words, Sarah Vowell knew what the man was really asking about—and it wasn't about art or the land. The man was looking for reasons to be optimistic *about the Bush administration.*

Stevie Wonder could see what was coming next.

Ms. Vowell says she attended President Bush's inauguration in 2001 and when he took the oath of office—ready for this?—she wept. Why? Well, because she was "terrified" that he would destroy the economy and "muck up my drinking water." The problem, she writes, is that she grossly underestimated George W. Bush's capacity to screw things up. "I lacked the pessimistic imagination to dread that tens of thousands of human beings would be spied on or maimed or tortured or killed or stranded or drowned, thanks to his incompetence.

"I feel like a fool. All those years of Sunday school, and still the apocalypse catches me off guard."

But there's no need for Ms. Vowell to feel like a fool. It's just the disorder talking. And here's the good news. People with Bush derangement syndrome don't know they have it. Just about everyone they know hates George Bush. And those are the only people they talk to inside their comfy little bubble. This is their universe. In it, they go about their lives telling each other that the apocalypse has arrived and that it's all the fault of that so-called president who stole that so-called election.

Being miserable, in a crazy kind of way, makes them happy. Global warming, I suspect, will make them downright ecstatic.

How the Religious Right (and Loony Left) Turned Barry Goldwater into a Liberal

In the Beginning...

When Barry Goldwater ran for president and was overwhelmingly defeated in 1964 (he won just six states: his own, Arizona, and five others, all in the Deep South), James Reston, the savvy Washington bureau chief of the *New York Times*, wrote the obituary: "Barry Goldwater not only lost the presidential election," he said, "but the conservative cause as well."

This may have been the first time, but certainly not the last time, the soothsayers at the *Times* would fail to understand the nature or the resilience of conservatism in America.

Like Ronald Reagan, who picked up the pieces and made conservatism a dominant force in American politics, Barry Goldwater was always comfortable being himself, even when it cost him votes. Toward the end of the 1964 campaign, for example, Goldwater visited a senior-citizen center in St. Petersburg, Florida, and told the old folks exactly what they did not want to hear: that he thought there should be some restraints on Medicare. Then he flew off to Knoxville, Tennessee, and did it all over again, this time wondering out loud about the wisdom of the TVA, the Tennessee Valley Authority.

At least the old guy believed in something and wasn't afraid to say it, which is more than we can say for a lot of his progeny in the Republican Party today.

As it turns out, Goldwater's brutal honesty may have scared off even more people than he realized. The day after his overwhelming defeat, the *Times* ran a story that quoted a conversation between two elderly women who had just voted. The first woman asked her friend if she had cast her eleventh-straight vote for the Republican candidate. No, the other woman said, this time she voted for the Democrat—Lyndon Johnson.

"Why?" her incredulous friend asked.

Because, came the reply, I was "afraid" to vote for Goldwater.

Why afraid, her friend asked.

"Because Goldwater will take away my TV."

"No, no, no," the other woman laughed. "Goldwater is opposed to the *TVA*, not TV."

"I know, I know," the friend said, "but I just didn't want to take any chances."

★

The fact is it wasn't just that old lady—and of course the media— who were afraid of Barry Goldwater. So were a lot of other Americans. The country wasn't ready for him or his conservatism back then. I sure as hell wasn't. (You may recall that several of my "open-minded," liberal college pals and I threatened to move to Australia if he won the '64 election.) Let's be honest: While there were plenty of good and decent folks who called themselves conservatives—Bill Buckley immediately comes to mind—the movement had more than its share of racists and anti-Semites. Goldwater wasn't a bigot, but the bigots were part of the movement. And no matter how honest and forthcoming the candidate may have been, the country simply was not ready to vote for anyone that conservative.

The good news, of course, is that we don't have to be captives of history. And, thank God, we're not. Conservatism, like liberalism, has transformed over the years. Except conservatism changed for the better. Today it's the Right that wants a color-blind America, while the Left wants color factored into all sorts of decisions they make. Today, Israel's biggest allies in America are conservative Christians. Its biggest enemies are intellectuals on the Left.

And now—as if to prove that history depends on who writes it—guess who the American Left has canonized as its newest folk hero? Guess who their newest icon is? Congratulations if you said "Barry Goldwater." Yes, *that* Barry Goldwater! The same one liberals used to detest and despise. Now they claim that Mr. Conservative underwent a transformation and before he died in 1998 became—miracle of all miracles—Mr. Liberal! Hillary Clinton and Ted Kennedy sing Goldwater's praises. Even the liberal lion himself, Walter Cronkite, has said, "I think he became a liberal."

You wish, Walter.

Yes, it's true that as he got older, Barry Goldwater did in fact become more liberal on social issues like abortion and gay rights. But to the end he remained what he always was: an individualist, a man of the old rugged West, a freethinking libertarian, the kind of conservative who wanted an intrusive government off his and all of our backs.

Still, liberals can believe whatever they want. It's a free country. And besides, the Left can use a few heroes who know how to ride a horse and fly a fighter plane.

But here's where things get *really* strange: It's not just liberals who say Goldwater became one of them. A lot of conservatives—Christian conservatives—agree with Hillary and Teddy and Uncle Walter. They also think Goldwater took a hard left late in his life. Except they think he went right off the road. How in the world could a real conservative, they wonder, embrace gay rights and abortion? As far as they're concerned, the liberals can have him.

Let's just say the feelings are mutual. As he got on in years, Barry Goldwater, who could be a cantankerous old coot, split with the Religious Right. "The Religious Right scares the hell out of me," he once said. "They should have no place in politics." He also urged all good Christians to "kick Jerry Falwell in the ass."

Which is why religious conservatives are returning the favor and kicking Goldwater, posthumously, in his libertarian ass. A lot of people on the Religious Right have written him off as a turncoat; a once-solid conservative who became a doddering old liberal fool; a traitor who late in life embraced the secularism of the Left. And most important, they see him as someone whose brand of libertarian conservatism—a brand that to this day doesn't especially take to mixing religion and politics—should be written out of the *future* of the Republican Party.

Ryan Sager, who has written a book called *The Elephant in the Room: Evangelicals, Libertarians, and the Battle to Control the Republican Party*, claims that Goldwater's distaste for the Religious Right was "far less the product of a shift in his views than a shift in the landscape of American politics."

"In short," Sager says, "the agenda of the social Right changed from keeping the government away from our nation's morality (opposing a ban on prayer in schools, opposing forced busing, opposing sex education) to insisting that the federal government be our moral arbiter (demanding money for faith-based initiatives, demanding abstinence education, demanding that a ban on gay marriage be written into the Constitution)."

There are important reasons, I think, that conservatives got feisty and started throwing their weight around. Liberals started it! Religious conservatives only became a political force after liberals began imposing *their* vision of morality on society. Liberals are the ones, after all, who thought it was a good idea for grade school kids to put condoms on bananas. So, evangelicals responded with their own version of sex in the classroom: lectures on abstinence. Same with same-sex marriage: Conservative Christians never thought about banning it until liberals came up with the idea of legalizing it. So, all religious conservatives have been trying to do is protect their own values from what they see as a liberal onslaught.

Except they responded not just with understandable outrage, but with a moral certainty of their own, one that was just as, if not more, fierce as the liberals'.

Both sides seem to have forgotten that this is a big country with 300 million people in it. We have different faiths and different religious values, and some Americans have no faith or religion at all. Conservatives are the ones who understand that government doesn't do very much very well. So, do they really want to call upon the messengers of government—the politicians and bureaucrats— to impose *on all of us* the kind of morality that is best left to the church and the privacy of individual lives? Do Christian conservatives really want that?

Years ago, a conservative named Frank Meyer, a senior editor at the *National Review*, said: "If the state is endowed with the power to enforce virtue, the men who hold that power will enforce their own concepts as virtuous." Exactly! And what happens when those men are liberal?

★

In the beginning there was Barry Goldwater, the man who helped shape the modern conservative movement in America; a man who said his philosophy was based on two ideas he learned as a boy growing up in the Arizona desert: respect of individual freedom and a belief that smaller government is a better government.

In those days, before air-conditioning, before the unifying forces of television and telephones and interstate highways, desert people developed a "rattlesnake toughness," as the locals like to describe it. The isolation made them more self-reliant than most; more independent, too. That's why Barry Goldwater became the man he was—the live-and-let-live, no-nonsense conservative. It's why he once told a newspaper reporter, "The conservative movement is founded on the simple tenet that people have the right to live as they please, as long as they don't hurt anyone else in the process."

Today there is a schism in Mr. Conservative's Republican Party—over many important issues, like nation-building in the hellhole that is Iraq, immigration, and yes, even religion. Now a lot of conservatives say the movement has strayed from the man who gave it its start in politics, and from his "get government off my back" conservative values.

I like conservative Christians. I like their decency. I admire their faith. I'm glad they vote the way they do. I understand why they're pro-life. And why they say, as a conservative Christian friend of mine said to me: Goldwater could have been a libertarian *and* pro-life; that when it comes to something as fundamental as protecting a human life, there's no contradiction in being both.

But just as I don't want liberals imposing their secular religion on me, I don't want people of faith using the power of government to impose their vision of morality on me, either. It's just not a good thing—not for a pluralistic country like ours. And besides, like Barry Goldwater, I've always been a little suspicious of people who think God really wants a bunch of pandering hacks in Congress to pass laws in His name.

Church, State, and Taxicabs in Minneapolis

I got a letter not long ago, asking for money. It began by telling me what a mess the world is in and how things are pretty crappy here in the United States, too.

There is a sense of "failure and despair" in the land, the letter said, right before ticking off all the injustices we need to correct.

There's the "health care crisis" the letter pointed out, "with a record 46 million Americans—including 10 million children—lacking any health insurance."

There's "the minimum wage that has not been increased since 1996."

There's "our dependence on foreign energy sources" and "global warming" that continue "to threaten our health and prosperity."

There's the "gap between the richest Americans and the poorest," which is nothing less than "a national scandal."

And finally there are those "challenges to abortion" and "to civil rights" and "to civil liberties."

At first I couldn't figure out how Nancy Pelosi got my name and address, since I haven't been on her team for quite a while now. But Nancy didn't send the letter. Neither did Howard Dean or Harry Reid or Ted Kennedy or any of the other liberal biggies. No, a rabbi sent it to me. A rabbi from a "progressive" organization called Reform Jewish Appeal.

For those who aren't members of the tribe, let me explain a few things about Reform Jews. They're the most liberal of the three major Jewish sects—Orthodox and Conservative being the other two. They live like Episcopalians and vote like Puerto Ricans, as the old saying goes. They have nothing in common with the no-frills Jews you'd see in *Fiddler on the Roof*. (Now, *they* were Jews!)

The letter didn't mention a single word about God or faith or any silly religious stuff like that, which is not all that surprising, since many liberal Jews consider themselves way too sophisticated to have faith in an invisible man who lives in the sky. But the letter did invoke the name of the prophet Isaiah in order to inform me that "our world is not working the way it is supposed to, not working the way it was meant to." What a coincidence! Isaiah wants exactly the same things as the Democratic National Committee. What are the odds?

Just one question: How, exactly, is bringing the prophet Isaiah into this, in order to raise the minimum wage, any different from the *dreaded* Religious Right using the Bible to justify its opposition to embryonic stem-cell research or gay marriage? I thought liberals wanted a giant wall separating church and state. Yet right there in the letter it says, "our Reform Jewish Movement has had a voice in Washington that speaks truth to power." Again, why is it kosher for liberal Jews to play footsie with politicians, but when the Religious Right does the exact same thing, it's the first step toward a Christian theocracy?

Frankly, I wish both sides would pay more attention to saving souls and less to getting legislation through Congress. For years, the Religious Right has mixed faith and Republican politics, invoking the name of God and turning Jesus into a precinct captain to push its evangelical agenda. The Religious Left—and by the way, when was the last time you heard *that* term on the evening news?—has signed on with the secular Democrats, who in case you haven't noticed, aren't all that secular anymore. Nancy Pelosi, the liberal

Democrat who in 2007 became Speaker of the House, once called on her colleagues to vote "no" on one of President Bush's budgets—"as an act of worship." Harry Reid, the Democratic majority leader in the Senate, has set up a Web site that he calls "Word to the Faithful." And liberal religious activists aren't shy about bringing Jesus—or Satan—in to help fight their political battles.

"I think [President Bush] should remember that it was the devil who tempted Jesus with unparalleled wealth and power" is how the late William Sloane Coffin, the Protestant minister and longtime left-wing political activist once put it in his denunciation of the president's "tax cuts for the rich." Funny, I thought only "dumb" conservative Christians dragged the Devil into political debates. Now the "sophisticated" Left is throwing Satan at us, too? If this isn't a sign that the end is near, I don't know what is.

Still, I certainly am not saying it's wrong for religious organizations to ever get involved in important political issues. I'm glad Christians and Jews fought for civil rights, to use one easy example. I'm glad, too, that the Reform Jewish Movement is working with politicians of both parties to try to end the atrocities in Darfur. Frankly, democracy needs those moral underpinnings that religion brings to the table.

The problem is that when churches of the Left *or* the Right bring the Bible into the debate, there is no debate. Every issue is black or white, right or wrong, good or evil. Run-of-the-mill partisan ideology gets all dolled up to look like a principled stand based on morality. And both sides *know* they're right, because God, or Jesus, or Isaiah told them so. *What's left to debate after that?*

In Minneapolis, God told Muslim taxi drivers at the airport not to pick up anyone carrying wine or liquor in their bags. The Koran—as they read it, anyway—forbids buying, selling, drinking, or carrying alcohol. So if the drivers see you with one of those transparent duty-free shopping bags with wine inside, or if you say,

"Please be careful with my luggage, there's a bottle of scotch in there," a lot of them won't pick you up. Allah told them not to. One driver said, "This is our religion. We could be punished in the afterlife if we agree [to transport alcohol]. This is a Koran issue. This came from heaven."

About 75 percent of the nine hundred cab drivers at the Minneapolis airport are Somali, and many of them are Muslim. So, the Muslim American Society's Minnesota chapter sent a *fatwa*—a religious edict—to the people who run the Minneapolis airport, which says "Islamic jurisprudence" prohibits taxi drivers from carrying passengers with alcohol, "because it involves cooperating in sin according to Islam."

No, this is not a *Seinfeld* episode.

So what does the Metropolitan Airports Commission do in the face of such behavior? Does it tell the Muslims that in a diverse, democratic society government doesn't embrace religious dogma; that it doesn't impose the rules of anybody's holy book onto its citizens; that it wouldn't tolerate a cab driver's "right" not to pick up Jews or gays or blacks on religious grounds and that it won't tolerate this either?

Dream on. This is America, where politicians of both major parties live in constant fear of coming down on the wrong side of some religious issue. So the Airports Commission devised a *brilliant* plan to appease the Muslims and their religious concerns: color-code the lights on the taxi roof to indicate whether a driver will accept a passenger carrying alcohol.

It was only because of overwhelming public reaction against the plan that it never actually went into effect. A spokesman for the Airports Commission said, "I think people were afraid there would be a chapter two."

In fact, chapter two has already kicked in. In several countries, Muslim cab drivers refuse to pick up blind customers with seeing-eye dogs, because the dogs are considered unclean. And as a wine-toting flight attendant who was refused service by a Muslim cab driver at the Minneapolis–St. Paul airport put it, "What's going to be next, do I have to cover my head?" Incredibly, a spokesman for the Airports Commission said that if other religious issues come up, they would be dealt with on a case-by-case basis.

But by early 2007, after more and more Muslim drivers refused to pick up passengers for religious reasons, the bureaucrats had come to their senses. That's when they decided to crack down on the Muslim taxi drivers—threatening to suspend their licenses for thirty days if they refused to pick up passengers. "Our expectation," a spokesman said, "is that if you're going to be driving a taxi at the airport, you need to provide service to anybody who wants it."

Despite the last-minute infusion of common sense, the Minneapolis airport saga is a pretty good example of why clearly religious issues should not come up in government in the first place. Leave them in church or the synagogue or the mosque. Otherwise, there's a danger that the ones with a pipeline to God will take over, a little at a time. And when they do, they'll dictate everything from taxicab rules to what we can and cannot do in our bedrooms to how much a waiter at Denny's should make. And they'll quote God or Allah or some Hebrew prophet to back up every last detail. Democracy depends on reason and compromise. Religion doesn't.

The Christian philosopher C. S. Lewis understood what could happen if the moralizers ever took over. "It may be better to live under robber barons than under omnipotent moral busybodies," he said. "The robber baron's cruelty may sometimes sleep, his cupidity may at some point be satiated; but those who torment us for our own good will torment us without end, for they do so with the approval of their consciences."

Political Science

Every Saturday morning I play basketball with a bunch of liberal Democrats and one conservative Republican, a born-again Christian named Rollie. After our games, four or five of us stay behind, sit down under a tree, and talk about the state of the world.

One Saturday I asked Rollie if he thought creationism, or Intelligent Design, should be taught in science class in our public schools. "Absolutely," he said, as the others rolled their eyes. "Look at this," he said, pointing to the trees and the grass and the sky. "You think all this evolved from a big bang?"

Instead of simply saying "As a matter of fact I do," I probed further, mostly because I knew how much this was annoying my liberal friends. "But what about science?" I asked him. "God is the greatest scientist of all," Rollie said, and he wasn't kidding.

At this point the libs shot me a look that said, "Thanks a lot, jerk-face, for getting this holy-roller going."

I like Rollie. I like the fact that he takes his religion seriously. I like the fact that he's a good family man, to use that much-overused phrase. I even like the fact that on the rare occasion when he misses an easy shot, he says, "Gosh darn it," instead of what the rest of us say. In a word, I like Rollie's decency.

But while I have a great deal of respect for his jump shot and his passion on the court, I am less than enthusiastic about his passion for injecting religion into the classroom and then pretending it's science. When the proponents of Intelligent Design argue that life is so complex that it must have been created by some higher force, that there must have been an "architect" behind the whole thing, what architect do you think they're talking about—Frank Lloyd Wright? Sorry, Darwin and Jesus cannot live side by side—not in science class anyway. If they want to teach this stuff in comparative religion class, or philosophy class, or even social studies, I have no problem. But I don't want creationism, Intelligent Design, or whatever they want to call it, taught to my daughter in science class—*because it is not science.*

Can you imagine the outcry if a history teacher got up in front of his class and told his students that Franklin Roosevelt was our first president and that he freed the slaves? Imagine if he told them the Civil War was fought in 1973.

Or if a math teacher told his kids that two and two equals nine. Or if an English teacher told her students that Ernest Hemingway wrote *Hamlet* in 1492.

No one would tolerate any of that! But somehow, because God is involved, we're supposed to pretend junk science is the real thing?

So who's the villain here? Not really the conservative Christians, who at least have the virtue of honestly believing they're doing the right thing. No, it's the politicians who are too weak to stand up to them and say, "Please keep your religion in your church, in your home, in your life. But keep it out of our schools."

A few born-again Democrats who are pushing creationism in school, but they're local politicians scattered here and there. The real culprits are conservative Republicans, and not just the local variety. The national Republican Party understands the politics of religion, or at least thinks it does. Party leaders know that evangelical ministers can mobilize their large congregations and turn out the vote for the GOP the same way that black churches can turn out the vote for Democrats. President Bush has even weighed in on the great debate, saying that public schools should present the concept of Intelligent Design along with evolution when teaching about the origins of life. As a religious man, maybe he really believes that evolution tells only part of the story. But as president, he has a higher responsibility: to ensure that religious doctrine isn't co-mingled with education content in public schools.

But who are we kidding? As a politician, he figures he can get points from conservative Christians when he says things like that, no matter how bogus and devoid of actual *science* they may be.

Pandering, after all, is what politicians do. But pandering when our children's future is at stake is reprehensible. It's a tough new world out there, one where national boundaries don't mean nearly as much as they used to, where our kids are going to have to compete with the smartest students on the planet. How does teaching pseudoscience help them—or the country—when students in India and China are learning *real* science?

If people of faith want to believe that God created the world six thousand years ago, because that's what the Bible tells them, fine with me—so long as they keep it in Sunday school. "To maintain a belief in a 6,000-year-old earth requires a denial of essentially all the results of modern physics, chemistry, astronomy, biology and geology," as the physicist Lawrence M. Krauss put it in a piece for the *New York Times*. "It is to imply that airplanes and automobiles work by divine magic, rather than by empirically testable laws."

Throughout history, governments have given in to the allure of pseudoscience and have paid a dear price for their ignorance. In the late 1920s, the Soviet Union adopted the crackpot agricultural theories of a screwball named Trofim Lysenko. Known as the "peasant scientist," he managed to convince Stalin and later Khrushchev—precisely because they were true believers in the infallibility of communism—that crops could be "trained" to serve Soviet agricultural interests, thereby miraculously expanding food production. The result was a man-made agricultural disaster of monumental proportions, which left millions of his countrymen dead or starving.

In the early 1930s, German physicists came up with their own brand of science, which they called "Deutsche Physik," literally "German physics" or "Aryan physics," which were nothing more than politically motivated, anti-Semitic weapons used to denigrate research done by Jewish scientists—dummies like Albert Einstein.

Today, Muslim fundamentalists think that Allah has all the answers, so who needs science? And while the modern world moves forward, they remain mired in their self-imposed Dark Ages.

I certainly don't mean to compare Christian fundamentalists with communists, Nazis, or Muslim fanatics. But could some less egregious, more American, form of this ideological nonsense take hold here? If we give pseudoscience a seat at the table with real science, it could. People of faith believe traditional scientific principles can never prove the greater truths they seek to reveal. So they look to the Bible for answers. And then they try to sneak the Bible into the classroom.

In 1999, the state school board in Kansas, which was dominated by creationists, expunged evolution from the state's science curriculum, much like the communists in the old Soviet Union expunged ideas they didn't like. Gone, too, was the big bang theory. How did the universe begin? Not with a bang—not in Kansas classrooms, anyway.

In 2004, in rural Dover, Pennsylvania, the local school board became the first in the nation to mandate the teaching of creationism's successor, Intelligent Design, in science class.

Other communities were moving in the same direction.

But in December 2005, a federal judge in Pennsylvania, whom the Associated Press described as "a Republican and a churchgoer," ruled that the Dover school-board policy on Intelligent Design was a "breathtaking inanity"—nothing more than "a religious view, a mere relabeling of creationism, and not a scientific theory." A month earlier, voters in Dover had come to the very same conclusion, ousting all eight pro–Intelligent Design school-board members who were up for reelection. In 2006, voters in Kansas ousted a pro-creationist majority from the state school board—including one member who said evolution was "an age-old fairy tale" and "a nice bedtime story" unsupported by science—replacing it with moderates who don't want creationism or Intelligent Design or anything else like it taught in the state's public schools.

If there's a message in all of this, it may be that voters—even religious voters—know when they're being condescended to. They don't like panderers. Most of all, they want their children to get a science education in science class—not pseudoscience, not faith-based science, and not *political* science, either.

That's the good news. The bad news is that the faithful have now moved beyond creationism and even beyond Intelligent Design. They're now peddling something called "creative evolution." I can't wait to see how the panderers will react to this one.

★ ★ ★ ★ ★ ★ ★ ★ ★ ★ ★ ★

Being Liberal Means Never Having to Say You're Sorry

A Witch Hunt in Durham

Every now and then all the pieces fall into place, or at least we're told they do. All the preconceived notions about race and class and privilege are validated by a single event, or at least we're told they are.

The "Duke Lacrosse Rape Case," as it came to be known, was a perfect morality play for the charter members of the elite liberal culture: the left-wing professors on campus who see oppression around every corner; the hard-core feminists who are constantly chattering about the "patriarchy" and how it subjugates women, especially women "of color"; the liberal news reporters who pride themselves on their skepticism, then devour every lie a rogue prosecutor feeds them; and the North Carolina civil rights establishment that would continue to demonize the three Duke students accused of rape no matter how clear the evidence was of their innocence.

The story was simply too juicy to let facts get in the way. Here they had a "crime" where the "victim" was a young, black single mother of two who was stripping in clubs and at private parties to pay the bills. And the "villains" were not only young white men but preppie jocks who played the rough-and-tumble game of lacrosse—and, worse yet, whose parents had money. And it was all happening in the South, where, as everyone was supposed to know, racial animus is ingrained in the culture.

It was too good to be true. And, as we all know by now, it really was. The whole story was a lie. There was no rape in the Duke Lacrosse Rape Case. In fact, there was no evidence linking the three lacrosse players to any sexual assault. None. Not a single shred.

Which is not to say there wasn't plenty of wrongdoing.

This time racial history and injustice in the South were turned upside down. This time the black woman who yelled rape was the liar. This time the corrupt district attorney went after white guys, who faced thirty years in prison, even though it was clear early on that the so-called "victim" was mentally unstable and had made the whole thing up. And this time the mob demanding vengeance for a crime that never happened wasn't made up of the usual bunch of yahoos. This time, the rabble salivating for a lynching was made up of those well-educated elites, those supposedly fair-minded liberals.

The biggest villain of all, of course, was Michael Nifong, the district attorney who was in the midst of a tight primary election when he went after the lacrosse players—and who desperately needed black votes to stay in office.

Nifong went on a media blitz in the days after the alleged rape, which supposedly took place at a lacrosse team party on March 13, 2006, calling the entire Duke team "a bunch of hooligans" and saying there was no doubt that the black dancer had been raped at the party. This even though she had changed her story about what happened that night over and over again, at first saying nothing about being raped, then claiming she had been gang-raped by twenty of the players, then changing the number to three. Even though a second stripper at the party said there was no rape. And even though the accuser had made similar accusations before, claiming in 1996 that three men had raped her, a charge she never pursued and one her own father told reporters was false. So determined was the district attorney to convict the lacrosse players in the court of public opinion that he once shamelessly went on MSNBC and theatrically demonstrated how one of them had choked Crystal Magnum, the stripper who made up the phony story.

Worse yet, Nifong concealed DNA test results from defense lawyers, tests that showed there was no contact—none!—between any of the players and the supposed "victim." None of it mattered to Mike Nifong. Dropping the case might have cost him those black votes he needed to win the election. As Stuart Taylor and KC Johnson put it in their book *Until Proven Innocent*: "The message was clear: Lynch the privileged white boys. And due process be damned."

For a while, Nifong's unscrupulous tactics worked to his benefit. In May 2006, he won the Democratic primary and in November he won the general election, both times with substantial support from Durham's black voters. But justice was coming, though not the kind Mike Nifong was expecting. By the end of 2006, his case was in a shambles. In April 2007, North Carolina Attorney General Roy Cooper concluded a long investigation and declared Nifong a "rogue prosecutor" and said that the Duke students were "innocent" and that he was dropping all charges against them. He also said that, because of her mental state, he would not file charges against the stripper who concocted the whole story.

On June 15, 2007, publicly disgraced and humiliated, Michael Nifong resigned. One day later, he was disbarred. And on September 7, he went to jail—but for only one day—for willfully lying to a judge about the exculpatory DNA evidence he had hidden from the defense.

But there was no day of reckoning for the many other villains in the Durham Witch Hunt, the liberal cultural elite who so willingly allied themselves with Michael Nifong.

There have been no apologies from the feminist student protestors who put pictures of Duke lacrosse players on their homemade "Wanted" posters, which they plastered all over campus; no apologies either from the ones who held rallies and waved banners screaming the word "castrate."

And there were no apologies from the left-wing professors who served as Mike Nifong's cheerleaders. Eighty-eight of them—who came to be known as the Group of 88—signed a statement saying "thank you" to the protestors for "not waiting" for charges to be filed before they went out and pronounced the players guilty. Houston Baker, who taught English and African-American Studies at Duke, called the players "white, violent, drunken men . . . veritably given license to rape, maraud, deploy hate speech." And while the radicals were trashing the concept of presumed innocence, the other professors sat by quietly, too afraid to open their mouths. According to Taylor and Johnson: "For many months *not one* of the more than five hundred members of the Duke arts and sciences faculty . . . publicly criticized the district attorney or defended the lacrosse players' rights to fair treatment. Not even after enough evidence had become publicly available to establish clearly both the falsity of the rape charge and the outrageousness of Nifong's actions—widely seen as the worst case of prosecutorial misconduct ever to unfold in plain view."

Richard Brodhead, the university president, was equally craven. He never supported the three young men, his own students, publicly or otherwise. And he not only canceled the entire lacrosse team season schedule but forced the resignation of Mike Pressler, the team's head coach, who, a university committee would later conclude, did absolutely nothing wrong. Brodhead was determined not to offend the racial and gender activists on his own faculty, prompting Bill Thomas, one of the defense lawyers, to say that "Brodhead lacked the courage to stand up and support these boys and their team in their moment of greatest need, and in my view hung them out to dry."

Even blacks who knew all about the awesome power of politically motivated white prosecutors hopped on the Nifong bandwagon and demanded the heads of the lacrosse players. At first, they understandably wondered why a white prosecutor—in the South, no less—would go after three young white men if they *weren't* guilty. But even as the suspicion rose that Nifong had oversold his case, many blacks refused to believe it. One African-American minister claimed "the moment they were accused" the players "should have been handcuffed; they should have been arrested; and the bail should have been set." A student at a historically black college in Durham told *Newsweek* that the players should be prosecuted "whether it happened or not. It would be justice for things that happened in the past." And Jesse Jackson chimed in too, saying "something happened" and promised that his Rainbow/PUSH Coalition would pay for Crystal Mangum's college tuition—even if it turned out that she lied about the rape.

Is this what Martin Luther King Jr. and the other heroes of the civil rights movement fought and died for—so innocent white men could be railroaded just as black men had been for so many years? "If the Duke lacrosse players were black," wrote Jason Whitlock, an African-American sportswriter for the *Kansas City Star*, "and the accuser were white, everyone would easily see the similarities between this case and the alleged crimes that often left black men hanging from trees in the early 1900s." But the liberal elite in Durham, black and white, closed their eyes both to the irony and the injustice that were unfolding before them. Like Nifong, they ignored any evidence that would derail their little morality play.

And the news media were no better. In the early days, they also had reason to believe the prosecutor. Why would he lie? And besides, they had before them a tantalizing story line, one that played on a long history of white men in the South preying on black women. That was more than enough for those supposedly tough reporters who normally question every syllable uttered by people in power.

Not only did they not ask the right questions; some didn't even get their facts straight. "There's something disgustingly wrong when a Duke University men's lacrosse team . . . puts some skewed code of silence ahead of telling Durham, N.C., police everything they know," said Johnette Howard, a sports columnist at *Newsday* in New York. But there was no code of silence. Several team captains voluntarily gave statements to police. They voluntarily gave DNA samples, and they volunteered to take polygraph tests, an offer the authorities rejected. The rest of the players said they would give their DNA for testing and answer any question the police had as long as they could have their lawyers present. This was not only their constitutional right, but a practical concern because the Durham police, like DA Nifong, had issued false statements about the case, saying there was no doubt that "a brutal rape" had occurred and that there was "really, really strong physical evidence" of rape—even though, in fact, there was absolutely no evidence at all.

When four captains issued a statement on March 28, 2006, saying that the rape charge was "totally and transparently false"; that the "team has cooperated with the police" and "provided authorities with DNA samples"; and that "the DNA results will demonstrate that these allegations are absolutely false," America's biggest circulation newspaper, *USA Today*, ignored the statement entirely in its March 30 edition.

And when DNA tests showed there was no link to any of the players, the *New York Times* put the story *not* on page one, where it had put so many of its pro-Nifong stories, but relegated it to the sports page.

The *Times*, which sets the agenda for so much of the national media, published more than a hundred news and opinion pieces on the Duke Lacrosse Rape Case, its first coming on March 29, 2006, just after Duke suspended the team's season. The story ran on page one, but incredibly never mentioned that Nifong was in the midst of a tough campaign for district attorney in a racially mixed city—the very catalyst, many believe, that motivated him to move forward with what turned out to be a disastrous and unjustified case.

Two days later, Selena Roberts, a *Times* sports columnist, rushed to judgment in a piece entitled "Bonded in Barbarity": "At the intersection of entitlement and enablement," she wrote, "there is Duke University, virtuous on the outside, debauched on the inside . . . a group of privileged players of fine pedigree entangled in a night that threatens to belie their social standing as human beings."

But not everybody at the *Times* was so willing to dismiss the presumption of innocence. Joe Drape, one of the paper's sports reporters, had been doing a fair job in the days after the case became public, presenting both sides of the story as best he could. At one point, Drape was working on a piece emphasizing the merits of the defense's case, but that article never made it into the paper. Drape reportedly told one of the defense lawyers that he was "having problems with the editors." And according to Taylor and Johnson: "Soon after Drape privately told people at Duke and, presumably, at the *Times* that this looked like a hoax, his byline disappeared from the Duke lacrosse story. The word among people at Duke and defense supporters, including one who later ran into Drape at a racetrack, was that the editors wanted a more pro-prosecution line. They also wanted to stress the race-sex-class angle without dwelling on evidence of innocence."

Which may explain why readers of the *New York Times* learned nothing about Michael Nifong's repeated refusals to look at evidence from the defense about the players' innocence, or why they learned nothing about the accuser's earlier claims of gang rape, or why they learned nothing about a case in 2002 in which she stole a taxi cab and led police on a high-speed chase. None of that fit the politically correct storyline.

Despite all this, the "public editor," or ombudsman, at the *Times* concluded that the paper's coverage was "basically fair." Defense lawyer Joe Cheshire didn't see it that away, not about the *Times* coverage and not about the media in general. "The authorities were leading the lynch mob, and the press was behind them clapping and screaming," he said. "It was stunning to see how they leapt to a conclusion, and their absolute unwillingness to listen to anything that wasn't what they had already decided they wanted to be true. What I've found out about those folks is that they're kind of in a way like Nifong. They're like bullies."

In the end, the bully, Michael Nifong, paid for his indifference to the truth. His many allies—in academia, in the civil rights establishment, and in the media—never did.

(In September 2007, though, three months after the case was thrown out, Duke president Richard Brodhead finally got around to apologizing for his "failure to reach out" to the lacrosse players. "The fact is that we did not get it right," he said, "causing the families to feel abandoned when they were most in need of support. This was a mistake," he admitted. "I take responsibility for it, and I apologize for it." You have to wonder, of course, whether this half-hearted apology was prompted by a nagging conscience or maybe by more mundane concerns over alumni disgust with his behavior—and, more importantly, how that might affect their generosity to the school.)

What these allies never understood (or didn't want to understand) was that the Duke Lacrosse Rape Case wasn't about the oppression of black women by white men, but rather about the astounding power of a reckless prosecutor. If Nifong was prepared to go after innocent, privileged, white boys for political gain, how far would he go to convict poor, innocent, black defendants if someday doing *that* fit his political purposes? It was an inconvenient question that never seemed to cross the mind of the liberal cultural elite, the ones who made such a travesty of justice in Durham possible.

The Passion of the Left

Mel Gibson says he's not a bigot. He says he's not an anti-Semite. I'm guessing he's mistaken on both counts. I'm old school. I think when you get drunk you get honest. Or at least you say the things you believe are honest. *"In vino veritas,"* the Romans used to say—in wine [is the] truth. In Gibson's case, it was tequila, but when he had too much of it, I think, the truth—Mel's truth—about those "f**king Jews" who "are responsible for all the wars in the world" came tumbling out. I don't think you say stuff like that, even if you're drunk, unless it's inside of you, someplace. But I can't say for sure what's in Mel Gibson's head, or in his heart. So let's be generous and say that he's a recovering anti-Semite, at least.

I say "recovering," because so far he's apologized about 42 million times. On ABC's *Good Morning America*, he told Diane Sawyer, "I'm ashamed [those words] came out of my mouth." Isn't that what we want from people who say bigoted things: remorse? Don't we want bigots—if that's what he is—to say, "I'm sorry"? But the Left just won't let go.

They won't let Mel Gibson off the cross even though, whatever else he may be, he's not a danger to Jews. He's not some thug in Nazi Germany in the 1930s making anti-Semitic comments that might very well have dire consequences. He's not a Muslim terrorist, either, who wants to kill Jews. He's not a leftist activist on campus who wants Israel eliminated from the face of the earth. He's an actor. And on that night in July 2006, he was a drunken actor who said stupid things. There's a tradition both in Judaism and Christianity that once someone apologizes, we forgive and move on. So why won't liberals forgive Mel Gibson?

Why, especially when you consider all the other people liberals forgive—people far, far worse than Mel Gibson. They forgive killers on death row all the time. They even turn some of them into celebrities. Years ago in New York, the liberal elites turned Jack Henry Abbott into a star; this was after he was convicted of murder. Norman Mailer, the Pulitzer Prize–winning author told the parole board what a wonderful writer Jack Henry Abbott was, and with the help of some of Mailer's liberal friends, they got him released from prison. Once free, he instantly became the guest of honor at many chic Manhattan dinner parties, dining with the kind of swells who find it exciting to sip wine and eat lamb with a cold-blooded killer. That went on for about six weeks, until Jack Henry Abbott made a little mistake. He killed somebody else. But even that wasn't enough for those hip liberals to give up on him. Shortly after his second conviction for murder, Susan Sarandon had a baby and, along with the father, actor Tim Robbins, named him Jack Henry.

More recently, the Los Angeles glitterati made a Hollywood star out of Stanley "Tookie" Williams, another cold-blooded killer. Tookie was one of the founding fathers of the Crips, the violent street gang responsible for several thousand murders in Los Angeles alone. One night, he went out on the town with a gun and murdered four innocent people, a crime that put him on death row at San Quentin and eventually caught the attention of the compassionate Left.

Tookie has changed, his many liberal supporters told anybody who would listen. He writes children's books. He preaches against gang violence. Without a hint of irony, or embarrassment, they even nominated him for a Nobel Peace Prize. And when all his appeals ran out and the state of California stuck a lethal needle in his arm, they wept for Tookie Williams, even though I'd bet anything that none of those liberals could name even one of the people he shot dead in cold blood that night.

But the compassionate Left won't forgive Mel Gibson for a drunken tirade?

Only liberals could devise a moral code in which bigotry—expressed only in words—is considered worse than murder.

But let's face it. Mel Gibson, despite the hand-wringing, is the best thing that has happened to liberals in a long time. He's their poster boy. The one they can point to whenever they need a little evidence to prove their most basic, dark, delusional belief about conservatives: that, like Mel, they're all racists, homophobes, anti-Semites, and all-around bigots—just like Bush and Rush and Fox News and all the other conservative bogeymen liberals like to call on when they need to make what passes for a point.

But shunning Gibson while they embrace killers makes sense at another level, too. Liberals, after all, define themselves by their compassion. So when they hold rallies and vigils for murderers—even when the killers have shown absolutely no remorse for their crimes—the Left gets to show off its virtue. This is how they tell the world how wonderful they are. It's how they proclaim their decency. It's how they show how much they care about the "downtrodden" and "oppressed" of society. In the end, this isn't about Mel Gibson at all. It's about liberals themselves. It always is when you're dealing with narcissists.

It's odd how people who are always going off on scavenger hunts, searching for "root causes" to explain whatever deviant behavior they happen to be championing at the moment—this killer had a father who beat him; that one had a mother on crack; they all grew up behind one eight ball or another—don't give a damn about Mel Gibson's root causes.

In October 2006, when he sat down with Diane Sawyer on *Good Morning America*, after apologizing a few more times, Gibson tried to explain where the anger came from the night the cops picked him up for driving drunk on the Pacific Coast Highway in Malibu.

He told Sawyer that he had been angry for quite some time about the shots he had taken—a lot of them from Jewish people—over his movie *Passion of the Christ*, which was blasted, in important places like the *New York Times*, as anti-Semitic. That, Gibson said, might have been the source of his drunken anti-Jewish tirade that night. "Even before anyone saw a frame of the film," he said, "for an entire year, I was subjected to a pretty brutal sort of public beating. During the course of that, I think I probably had my rights violated in many different ways as an American. You know, as an artist, as a Christian. Just as a human being, you know." Then, he added, the film came out and none of the terrible things that liberals had predicted happened. There were no attacks on Jews at all. To the contrary, many Christians reached out to Jews. "It was released, and you could have heard a pin drop, you know. Even the crickets weren't chirping," he told Sawyer. "But the other thing I never heard was one single word of apology."

Is that an excuse for slandering Jews? No. But it might explain why he said what he said when he got drunk. The fact that he grew up with a Holocaust-denying father might explain some of it too. But none of it mattered to the liberals who despised him. Geraldo Rivera, who is half Jewish and all liberal, went on the air with Bill O'Reilly and expressed the views of many in the liberal entertainment culture: "Mel Gibson is a creepy, sniveling anti-Semite." He said this, by the way, *after* Gibson's very public media culpa on *Good Morning America*. Root causes apparently only count sometimes with liberals.

At one point during his interview with Diane Sawyer, Gibson said he wanted to make a statement right to the camera. "Let me be real clear here, in sobriety, sitting here, in front of you, on national television, that: I don't believe that Jews are responsible for all the wars in the world. I mean that's an outrageous, drunken statement."

Yes, it is. A reflection, I think, of Mel Gibson's problem with Jews. But if liberals can show compassion for brutal murderers and supposedly oppressed terrorists—if they can try to make sympathetic victims out of *them*—then surely they can find a little compassion for a man who has killed no one and has said "I'm sorry" over and over and over again. If they can't, then it tells us more about liberals than it does about Mel Gibson. A lot more.

So what would it take for liberals to finally forgive Gibson? Well, for openers, it would help if he renounced his conservative politics. That would make him a lot more likable to the Left. After that, all he'd really need to do is find some vicious unapologetic murderer on death row, nominate him for the Nobel Peace Prize, and try to get him out of prison. That would really show Mel Gibson's decency—at least as far as compassionate liberals are concerned.

Change the Channel

Whenever I complain to my liberal friends about the raunchiness on network television, they roll their eyes and say, "Hey, if you don't like it, change the channel."

I explain that I'm not a prude. I don't care what people do in their *private* lives. I don't care how they talk and I don't care if they sit around the house all day watching porn. I don't care what they watch on HBO or Showtime, either. Adults pay for that. But sex jokes about three-ways, during what we used to call the family hour, on network sitcoms is another matter. That's the *public* arena. I tell them that this stuff offends a lot of good people in America, even if it doesn't bother my "sophisticated" liberal friends. To which they reply: "Change the channel."

"We're supposed to care about the environment," I say. "So what about the cultural environment? Doesn't that matter?"

"No," they say. "Change the channel."

But even if I change the channel, I try to explain, it's still out there polluting the culture: the simulated sex scenes, the adulterous affairs, the junior high sex jokes about the guy who goes to sleep "jerkin' his gherkin and wakes up every morning humping his mattress" (as one character put it on *Dawson's Creek*), and the plots about mothers having sex with their high school daughter's ex-boyfriends. *And it's all aimed at kids!*

No, it's not as bad as terrorism. I readily acknowledge that. But that doesn't mean it's good. And crummy as these shows are, I tell my friends, I don't want the morality police to shut them down. All I want is a conversation about the impact this stuff has on society. Isn't what we watch (and especially what kids watch) for hours and hours every day on television important enough for a serious discussion that goes beyond "If you don't like it, change the channel"? To which they respond, "If you don't like it, change the channel."

I give up. I'm obviously getting nowhere. In fact, I'm so beaten down I'm even willing to accept that maybe I really am taking this stuff too seriously. Why not just change the channel? It's only television, right?

So, all my sophisticated liberal friends, let's try a little experiment. Imagine you're sitting on an airplane next to a well-dressed man who tells you he's an executive with CBS Entertainment.

"That's interesting," you say, "what's new on the fall lineup?"

"We've got a great comedy to anchor Monday night," he tells you. "It's called *Homo Say What?*"

You stare at him blankly, and he launches into it.

"It's sort of like *Will & Grace*, but different. It's about a couple of gay guys, and about all the funny little things that happen to them."

Rule #1 of air travel: Never talk to the person sitting next to you, because he may go on forever and there's no getting off the plane when it's flying at 36,000 feet. But it's too late now. So, even though you're not at all sure you want to know, you ask your neighbor, "What kind of funny little things?"

"Well," he tells you, "one of the homos—that's what they're called in the show, 'homos'—is a black guy named Cadillac, who's on welfare and just sits around the house all day watching television. The other homo, his boyfriend, is a Muslim named Mohammar Bruce. He's a full-time interior decorator and part-time pedophile, who likes painting the toenails of little boys he finds in the park.

"So one day the Muslim homo gets picked up by the cops—two corrupt Puerto Ricans who can barely speak English—for the toe-nail thing. This part is hilarious," he informs you. "The gay Muslim, in a very swishy high-pitched voice, says: 'If you don't let me out of here I'll blow up the police station—or paint it a really ugly color.'

"Then the Muslim guy says, 'I know my rights: Get me a lawyer. And make sure he's a Jew lawyer.' So the Jewish lawyer, whose nose is bigger than the Washington Monument, comes down to the jail, slips the crooked cops a few bucks, springs his client, and tells Bruce: 'Pay me, *in cash*. I'm a Jew. I don't want to report any of this on my taxes.'

"Anyway, when he gets home, Mohammar Bruce and Cadillac start talking to each other—except Bruce is speaking some Arab lingo and Cadillac is talking in Ebonics. Neither homo understands what the other one is saying.

"The next-door neighbor," he continues, "is a nymphomaniac midget lady who stutters. She's always coming on to the gay guys but can't figure out why they're not interested. One day she says to them, 'Is it because I'm vertically challenged?' It takes her ten minutes to get the word "vertically" out of her mouth, because she's stuttering so much. The gay guys are laughing their heads off.

"Oh yeah, the Muslim homo is a little hard of hearing and every time the nymphomaniac midget asks him if he wants to do it, 'or what,' the Muslim says '*What?*' Which is why we're calling the show *Homo Say What?*

"You love it, right?"

All you can do is stare—for a very long time.

Then you unload on the guy. You ask if he has any sense of decency; any sense of how this kind of stuff will offend millions of good people. You wonder if he has a clue about the impact this kind of trash will have on a culture that is already more than a little frayed around the edges. You blurt out the word *despicable*, and you open your newspaper to let him know the conversation is officially over.

But nothing you've said has made a dent. He doesn't understand why you're upset. "You're taking this way too seriously," he tells you with a bored look on his face. "It's only television." Then he dismisses you with one final thought:

"If you don't like it, change the channel."

Survive This!

As I write this in September 2006, liberals are up in arms. They're in an all-hands-on-deck, red-alert, full-scale tizzy. They're mad as hell and they're not going to take it anymore. Why? *Survivor*, the CBS television reality show, has divided its teams by race and ethnicity. There's a white team, a black team, an Asian team, and a Hispanic team.

How could they?

Asian-American New York City councilman John Liu is fuming. "The show has the potential to set back our nation's race relations by fifty years," he says.

Lisa Navarrette, a spokeswoman for the Latino civil rights group La Raza, is *muy* angry, too. "Are the producers utterly clueless about issues, or are they utterly soulless in that they're willing to engage this issue for the sake of ratings and buzz? It is really unconscionable and irresponsible."

Ray Richmond of the *Hollywood Reporter* agrees that it's a throwback to America's racist past. "All [Mark] Burnett [the show's creator and executive producer] had to do was give his baby a little bit of that Birmingham, Alabama, 1961 feeling to restore its luster in the popular consciousness."

A professor at Northwestern University, Lawrence Lichty says it's "a step backward"—one that "sure sounds dangerous to me."

On blackprof.com, professor Marc Hill writes, "If the folks at

CBS want to use 'Survivor' to talk about race, they should figure out how Black people manage to survive with inadequate health care, diminishing job opportunities, poor schools, and institutionalized racism."

On the Television page at Netscape, someone who calls himself "seaflight" wonders whom else the *Survivor* producers are going to segregate—"the invalids from the pure Aryan white race?" Disgustedly, he asks, "What's next?"

What's next? How about dividing people by race and ethnicity and then giving them extra points for being black or Hispanic and calling it college-admission affirmative action?

How about all-black college dorms?

How about dividing people by race, then handing out government contracts based on their skin color and ethnicity?

How about establishing a Hispanic public school, like La Academia Semillas del Pueblo in Los Angeles, where they teach "Aztec Math" and the Mexican indigenous language, Nahuatl—just to make sure Latino-American kids stay Latino and don't get too American?

Or how about setting up entire school districts based on race and ethnicity, just as the Nebraska legislature did, when it created three school districts in Omaha—one for whites, one for blacks, and one for Hispanics?

Why in the world liberals are upset over *Survivor* is way beyond me, since the show represents everything they stand for. Liberals love dividing by race and gender. They love bean-counting based on ethnicity and skin color. If some dopey conservative has the gall to say we should strive for a color-blind America, liberals say "color-blind" is code for "racism." *Survivor*'s producers say (with a straight face) they're not separating whites and blacks and Asians and Hispanics just to gin up the ratings. They say they're doing it for "diversity." Last time I checked, liberals loved diversity. They worship diversity. They think America is a better place because of diversity. So why is diversity such a bad thing all of a sudden?

"What's next?" our disgusted liberal friend asks. What's next is already here. It's a reality show that divides people into separate groups based on their race and ethnicity. It's called *America*.

W's Catch-22

Being liberal means never having to say you're sorry.

It means you can slander Ronald Reagan as the kind of crazy cowboy who would drag us into World War III, then never say a word when he ends the Cold War and helps liberate millions of Europeans who had been under the Soviet Union's thumb.

It means you can fight welfare reform tooth and nail, then say nothing when it gives millions of poor Americans dignity by taking them off the dole and putting them into the workforce.

It means you not only can excuse, but actually embrace, a dictator like Fidel Castro, then look the other way when he jails anyone who disagrees with him.

Most of all, being liberal means you can leave a whole lot of wreckage along the side of the road and never peek into the rearview mirror, because your intentions are good and your heart is in the right place.

Which brings us to our current war on terror.

If there's another terrorist attack on U.S. soil, there's one thing you can be sure of: Liberals, once again, will take no responsibility. They will be too busy blaming George W. Bush for whatever happens. They will blame him if he's still president. And they will blame him if he's been out of office for thirty-five years. Take it to the bank.

In fact, George Bush is caught in a kind of catch-22. If we *are* attacked, liberals will point to his "reckless" policies in Iraq and other parts of the world, which "emboldened" the terrorists, who, of course, otherwise would never have dreamed of attacking us (again). And if we're *not* attacked . . . well, how dare that SOB spy on us and take away our civil liberties?

There's no way liberals will ever let him out of this catch-22. Not just because blaming Bush is one of their most enduring sources of entertainment—and by extension blaming Cheney, Rove, Rumsfeld, Rice, Limbaugh, O'Reilly, Hannity, and the whole damn neocon universe right down to Ted Nugent and Bo Derek—but also because it conveniently takes the blame off of *them*. For instance, if there is another attack, liberals will be sure *not* to pin any responsibility on the *New York Times*, even though the paper has revealed sensitive government secrets aimed at foiling terrorist plots. They won't even acknowledge the *possibility* that by publishing those secrets the *Times may* have made us more vulnerable.

And if there's another attack involving airplanes, you can bet your life the Left won't take any blame for opposing ethnic profiling at airports. Instead, they will blame George W. Bush for not insisting on ethnic profiling. They'll also blame him for not catching the terrorists before they got anywhere near the airport.

Should there be another terrorist attack, you better believe liberals won't be shouldering any responsibility for their opposition to just about every other tough measure designed to fight terrorism—an intransigence that shows a great ignorance of history. Lincoln, whom many consider the greatest of our presidents, suspended all sorts of civil liberties during the Civil War, in order to save the country. He interfered with free-speech rights, with press rights, and he even suspended the right of *habeas corpus*, which meant that American citizens could be arrested and held without formal charges being brought against them. And exactly what long-term harm did any of that do? Now, the Left frets about a provision in the Patriot Act, which allows federal agents to snoop on what books a suspected terrorist is checking out of the library. The ACLU sees this as the first step to establishing a police state.

Then there's eavesdropping on suspected terrorists' phone calls and reading their e-mails without a warrant. This is a very important issue for the Left. But as the scholar James Q. Wilson pointed out in the *Wall Street Journal*, "Customs agents have the right to search without a warrant, you and your luggage (including your PC) when you enter this country. The Border Patrol can stop and search recent arrivals here when they are miles from the border. The Supreme Court has authorized customs officers to open incoming international mail without a warrant. It is not clear how a phone call or email originating overseas deserves more protection than clothing, the contents of a computer, or international mail. The Supreme Court has upheld all of these exceptions to constitutional limits on searches."

If there is another 9/11—or worse—liberals will insist, "We were just trying to protect everybody's constitutional rights." Expect no mea culpas from the Left. Liberals, after all, are virtuous by definition. Which is why they never bear responsibility for the consequences of their actions. As far as they're concerned, nothing else needs to be said.

But let's say it anyway: If there is another terrorist attack on Americans, lots more reasonable Democrats will move to the right and enthusiastically support George Bush and his war on terror. A conservative, don't forget, is a liberal who's been mugged by reality, as the saying goes. But rest assured that the true believers will never budge. In their world, George Bush is worse than the terrorists. That's their story and they're sticking to it.

This Just In . . .

I always thought that Lanny Davis, the liberal
Democrat who used to work for President Clinton and who pops
up on cable television all the time, was a decent, reasonable, and
smart man. I guess two out of three ain't bad.

It seems that Lanny isn't nearly as smart as I thought he was.
Turns out he has just made a shocking discovery that has shaken
him to his very core. Lanny Davis has just now learned that his fellow liberals can be really mean, nasty, vicious bastards.

Until this blinding light came out of nowhere and hit Lanny
Davis right between the eyes, like most liberals he thought that only
conservatives were really mean, nasty, vicious bastards.

In an August 8, 2006, *Wall Street Journal* op-ed titled "Liberal
McCarthyism," Davis wrote, "My brief and unhappy experience
with the hate and vitriol of bloggers on the liberal side of the aisle
comes from the last several months I spent campaigning for a longtime friend, Joe Lieberman. . . .

"This kind of scary hatred," he writes, "my dad used to tell me,
comes only from the right wing—in his day from people such as the
late Sen. Joseph McCarthy, with his tirades against 'communists
and their fellow travelers.' The word 'McCarthyism' became a red
flag for liberals, signifying the far right's fascistic tactics of labeling
anyone a 'communist' or a 'socialist' who favored an active federal

government to help the middle class and the poor, and to level the playing field."

It always goes back to our childhood, doesn't it? You learn something from your parents and it sticks with you all your life. Sometimes you learn that black people are inferior. Sometimes that Jews run the world and start all the wars. And sometimes you learn from your sweet dear old dad that "scary hatred . . . comes only from the right wing." So how can we fault poor Lanny for seeing conservatives as scary haters, too—and for thinking they have a monopoly on ugliness?

"I came to believe that we liberals couldn't possibly be so intolerant and hateful, because our ideology was famous for ACLU-type commitments to free speech, dissent and, especially, tolerance for those who differed with us. And in recent years—with the deadly combination of sanctimony and vitriol displayed by the likes of Rush Limbaugh, Ann Coulter and Michael Savage—I held on to the view that the left was inherently more tolerant and less hateful than the right."

Never mind that he's dead wrong about Limbaugh, Lanny Davis is going to tell us about his journey from the liberal bubble into the real world. "Now," he writes, "in the closing days of the Lieberman primary campaign, I have reluctantly concluded that I was wrong. The far right does not have a monopoly on bigotry and hatred and sanctimony."

Better late than never, I guess. Though you would have thought that someone in his early sixties, who went to Yale College and then to Yale Law School and who served as special counsel to a president of the United States, would have figured that out a long time ago. So, what exactly was it that caught Lanny Davis's eye? He gives us a few examples of postings on liberal Web sites:

"Everybody knows, Jews ONLY care about the welfare of other

Jews," one blogger wrote. Another said, "Lieberman cannot escape the religious bond he represents. Hell, his wife's name is Haggadah or Muffeletta or Diaspora or something you eat at Passover." Still another said, "Joe Lieberman is a racist and religious bigot." One more wrote that "Ned [Lamont] needs to beat Lieberman to a pulp in the debate and define what it means to be an American who is NOT beholden to the Israeli Lobby."

"And those," Davis writes, "are some of the nicer examples."

Indeed they are, Lanny—certainly nicer than what a lot of your liberal friends have been saying about conservatives for many, many years now. Are we really supposed to believe that Lanny Davis has never been to one of those sophisticated dinner parties in George-town or Manhattan or Martha's Vineyard where liberals sip wine and call George Bush a fascist; or where conservatives who are against affirmative action are called racists; or where anyone who opposes even late-term abortion is a woman-hating Neanderthal; or where disgusted Americans who want to put a fence up on the border to keep illegal aliens out are called jingoistic bigots?

And are we also supposed to believe that Lanny Davis has never heard the term "liberal hate speech"? It's been part of the vocabulary for quite some time now. Didn't he know that Nina Totenberg, the NPR reporter, went on one of those Sunday TV talk shows years ago and said, "If there is retributive justice, [Senator Jesse Helms] will get AIDS from a transfusion, or one of his grandchildren will get it."

Didn't the language bother him when Evan Thomas of *Newsweek* referred to Paula Jones as "some sleazy woman with big hair coming out of the trailer parks"?

Wasn't he troubled when left-wing pundit Julianne Malveaux said she hoped Clarence Thomas's wife "feeds him lots of eggs and butter and he dies early like many black men do, of heart disease," because he was "an absolutely reprehensible person"?

Or how about when Linda Ronstadt compared the Bush administration to "a new bunch of Hitlers"?

And this is the stuff they say in *public*!

I'm guessing Lanny wasn't troubled by any of it. Not all that much, anyway. I'm also guessing that he isn't nearly as clueless about liberal venom as he purports to be. It's just that in Lanny Davis's world there's intolerance and then there's intolerance. When the nasty shots are fired at "right-wingers," that's one thing. But when they're aimed at *good* people—at liberals like Joe Lieberman—well, that's something else altogether.

Frankly, Lanny, I'm glad those vicious liberals came after you and Lieberman. I'm glad their tirades—free of anything resembling intellect and reason—gave you the impetus to finally pull your head out of the sand and speak out against them. But if you continue to play deaf, dumb, and blind when your liberal pals spew their mindless venom at conservatives, then you will have learned absolutely nothing from this whole thing. And that, Lanny, would make you no better than the intolerant, sanctimonious haters your father warned you about.

Good Jew,
Bad Jew

I was the guest on a radio show in Knoxville, Tennessee, talking about how the culture has gotten too mean and nasty, when a caller tells me that he agrees with me. Then he pretty much tells me he thinks I'm a good Jew—compared to Barbra Streisand, who he thinks is a bad Jew.

Neither the host nor I had uttered so much as a syllable about religion up to that point. We had been talking about a book I had written, *100 People Who Are Screwing Up America*. Ms. Streisand was on my list of screwups—not, if it even needs to be said, because she's Jewish—but because of some of the crazy liberal things she's mouthed off about over the years. The caller didn't quite get that and felt it was perfectly okay, in this day and age, to announce which Jews he liked and which ones he didn't.

As far as he was concerned, he was just paying me a compliment.

But don't go thinking, "Well, what do you expect from Tennessee!" That would be unfair to all the good people in the state. It would also show a great deal of naïveté about what lots of people in the rest of the United States think about the Jews.

When it looked like there might be an all-out war in the Middle East in the summer of 2006, a caller on a national radio talk show seriously suggested that if the Israelis really want peace, they should give the entire country to the Palestinians and move to Australia.

Another caller thought Israelis were the real terrorists over there. "They blow up Arab houses," she said, "don't they?" Yes, they do. But only after Arab terrorists blow up civilians on buses and in restaurants, an inconvenient fact that had never made it to her radar screen.

Then there's C-SPAN. I used to think the people who watched C-SPAN were a cut above. Talk about naive! I was watching one of their call-in shows—the subject was Senator Joe Lieberman's support for the war in Iraq—and a critic of the war dialed in and said, "Al Gore ran with that Jew." On another day, a C-SPAN caller ticked off the names of Jewish journalists in the United States to explain (incredibly) why Palestinians, in his delusional view, get the short end of the stick in our mainstream media.

Nobody I talked to on the radio in Knoxville was that nasty.

It's not exactly that I'm shocked. Anti-Semitism, blatant and subtle, after all, has been around for quite a while. I'll never forget the story my parents told me, about when they went to a park in New Jersey in the late 1930s but couldn't get in. It must have been run by some private agency, because the sign at the gate said, NO DOGS AND NO JEWS ALLOWED. That was a long time ago, and to be perfectly honest, I haven't seen much anti-Semitism in my own life.

It seems, however, that there's something new going on out there. Something a friend calls "trickle-down bigotry." You've heard of trickle-down economics. The ones at the top make money and then some of it trickles down to the rest of the folks below. It's the same with trickle-down bigotry, he says. People at the top—respected people with important jobs, actually—say nasty things about Jews and before you know it, lots of ordinary people feel comfortable spouting off about good Jews and bad Jews, and about that Jew who ran with Al Gore, and telling Jews who spent their whole lives in Israel to pack their bags and move to Australia.

Before we go too far, let me acknowledge that some Jews are paranoid about anti-Semitism; mostly older ones who grew up with it. I understand their fears, but I don't share them. There's no place on the planet, outside of Israel, where Jews are more welcome than right here in America. This is one place where Jews can feel safe. Sure, in a nation of 300 million people you're going to find some bigots—the kind who think Jews are trying to control the world—but so what? Over the years, they've been isolated. Anti-Semitism just isn't as fashionable as it used to be.

Except in some circles.

Once, the right wing in this country had a monopoly on Jew-bashing. You expected it from the Ku Klux Klan, the neo-Nazis, and other assorted idiots like the ones who didn't want Jews in their precious little parks. But over the years things have gotten better for Jews. Much better. Today anti-Semitism, at least publicly, is simply not accepted—*not by respectable people*. Like most forms of blatant bigotry, it's in the domain of the uneducated. It's considered low-class.

Which is why the new anti-Semitism is so, well, interesting. This time around, it's coming from some high-class places and from some well-educated people. This time it's coming *not* from the right wing, but from the left wing—from left-wing intellectuals, of all people, on some of our finest American college campuses. And whether or not this new *respectable* anti-Semitism is actually trickling down to the people who call C-SPAN and talk radio shows or just mumble to their friends about "the Jews," this much seems certain: The new anti-Semites are giving the old anti-Semites a kind of legitimacy. They're giving them cover.

But anti-Semitism, they say, has nothing to do with it. Their target is Israel, they insist, not Jews.

I used to argue with friends who worried about the new anti-Semitism. I used to say these intellectuals aren't anti-Semites; they're just liberals, rooting for the underdog, which is what liberals always do—in this case, Palestinians and other Arabs. I used to argue that these same leftists once liked tiny, little Israel—*before* it became so powerful. In other words, there was a time when I thought Jews were confusing criticism of Israel—misguided and uninformed as it was—with anti-Semitism. But I've changed my mind. The rhetoric and the hypocrisy have simply gone too far.

They say they're arguing about policy, but then they call Israelis the new Nazis.

That's not how you argue policy. And at some of our best colleges—places like Harvard, MIT, Columbia, and Yale—they draw up campus petitions urging Americans not to invest in Israel and to actually *divest*, to pull all their money out in order to punish Israel. Of all the despicable countries in the world, why is it Israel—the only Jewish nation on earth—that gets them so worked up? Do they circulate petitions protesting Syria's human rights abuses, or those of despotic regimes in Africa? Is Israel the only "oppressor" worth their time and attention?

★

It sure looks that way. In 2002, Columbia University brought over Professor Tom Paulin, a prominent British poet from Oxford University, to teach in the English department for a semester. Never mind that earlier that same year, the good professor Paulin had told an Egyptian newspaper that Jewish settlers from New York who were living on the West Bank "should be 'shot dead.'" Never mind that he called them "Nazis" and "racists." Never mind, either, that he said, "I feel nothing but hatred for them." And just in case anyone missed his point, Professor Paulin went on to say, "I can understand how suicide bombers feel. . . . I think attacks on civilians in fact boost morale." (For the record, Paulin said his remarks were distorted, that he does not support attacks on Israeli civilians. But he has never disowned other statements about how Israel is "an historical obscenity" that has "no right to exist at all.")

And while Paulin was teaching at Columbia, the faculty of the English department at Harvard invited him to speak there—supposedly about his poetry. But when word got out that he was coming, anti-Paulin protests were planned, and Harvard *disinvited* him. This, as you might imagine, enraged more than a few "free speech" liberals on campus, and before you could say "McCarthyism is back," Paulin was invited to speak at Harvard yet again.

Ruth Wisse, who teaches at Harvard, says that some of our finest universities, including her own, "have gone out of their way to invite speakers best known for their defamation of Israel and the Jews."

In fact, in 2006, Harvard invited Mohammad Khatami, the former president of Iran, to speak on campus. This is a man who, when he's in places like the United States, claims to be a "moderate"—even though he ruled over a country that would like nothing better than to see Israel and every Jew in it wiped off the face of the Earth; a country where Holocaust denial is considered an intellectual pursuit. As then Massachusetts Governor Mitt Romney put it, Khatami is "someone who is without question a person who calls himself a moderate but at best is a moderate terrorist. And there's no such thing as a moderate terrorist. . . . This is a person who should not be welcomed to the United States, who should not be feted by Harvard University or any other university."

That this is happening on our college campuses is telling. These are politically correct liberal places, after all, that go out of their way to discourage ugly speech against minorities. Yet when Tom Paulin's presence at Columbia started to cause a rumble of protest, one professor contended that Paulin's comments "did not step over the line." Well, if saying Jews on the West Bank should be "shot dead" is not crossing the line, then what is?

And here we have a valuable lesson, I think, on how *gradualism* works. The radical hard-Left starts the Jew-bashing, mainly to show its devotion to "underdogs" and its hatred of "oppressors"—and others on the Left—*reasonable* liberals—quietly accept it as no big deal. At Oxford, some of Professor Paulin's colleagues used to say, "Well, that's just Tom being Tom." Then many of those *reasonable* liberals move from simply being passive, what's-the-big-deal bystanders to active defenders of hate speech, which is nothing less than fascinating, since they're the ones who are always lecturing everybody else on the horrors of hate speech. Now it suits them to argue that a call for mass murder of civilians "did not step over the line."

These are the crazies we need to be concerned about—not just the *radical* leftists, but also those *mainstream* liberals who once would have stood up against Paulin's vile ruminations *in the name of liberalism*—but now can't distinguish between "free speech" and an apparent incitement to kill innocent civilians. As an editorial in the *New York Observer* put it, "America's colleges and universities are allowing anti-Semitism to flourish under the guise of academic freedom. It's time to recognize this disease and to fight it. Are there no responsible scholars left in the Ivy League?"

★

I'd like to be very clear and state the obvious: People have every right to criticize Israeli policies. To do so does not make you a bigot. People have the right to question the power of the Jewish lobby in this country, and ask what influence it has on our government. That's all legitimate. But when the hard Left continually bashes Israel, *using the most inflammatory language*—and says far, far less about other countries, whose human rights records are far, far worse—then you have to wonder if this is simply legitimate debate or just old-fashioned Jew-bashing dressed up to look respectable.

I think Mort Zuckerman, the media mogul, is on to something when he says, "Israel has become the Jew among nations. It is both the surrogate—the respectable way of expressing anti-Semitism—and the collective Jew." But then Mort is a Jew himself, some of those professors might say, so how seriously should we take anything he says about Israel?

Actually, there's plenty of evidence to suggest Zuckerman is right. For example, world-class Israel-basher Noam Chomsky, the left-wing scholar from MIT—a man of Jewish heritage himself—combined his revulsion for Israel and his contempt for American Jews who support Israel in one simple sentence. They "get their psychological thrills from seeing Israel, a superman, stomping on people's faces," he said.

In May 2002, Jewish students at San Francisco State University held a Peace in the Middle East rally. As it ended, while some Jewish students were praying, pro-Palestinian students rushed into the plaza shouting, "Get out or we'll kill you" and "Hitler didn't finish the job."

When French synagogues were set on fire at the height of the Palestinian intifada in 2003, Tony Judt, a professor at New York University, said these were not incidents of anti-Semitic arson. Instead, he excused them as "misdirected efforts, often by young Muslims, to get back at Israel."

In October 2004, Duke University hosted a Palestine Solidarity Movement conference, which brought together various groups that had refused to condemn violence against Israeli civilians. One day after the conference ended, the student newspaper ran an op-ed by Philip Kurian, a Duke senior, which was simply titled "The Jews." Kurian apparently was not pleased with the criticism leveled against the conference by "the powerful Jewish establishment." And he wasn't too happy with "the Jews" themselves. "Jews," he wrote, "enjoy shocking overrepresentation" on America's college campuses. He also said that Jews have an advantage over other minorities. They "can renounce their differences by taking off the yarmulke."

And on July 28, 2006, a Muslim-American forced his way into the offices of the Jewish Federation of Greater Seattle and shot five people, killing one. "These are Jews, and I'm tired of . . . our people getting pushed around by the situation in the Middle East," the killer reportedly told a 911 operator. Was this also some "misdirected effort to get back at Israel"?

Of course, Americans of left-wing intellectual persuasion aren't alone when it comes to Israel-bashing. Europeans are really good at it, too—but then being anti-Jewish over there has a long, rich, miserable history. Tom McGurk, a writer in Ireland, has compared Israeli behavior to "Nazi-style barbarism."

The Greek composer Mikis Theodorakis, who has called Jews "sly," has also said: "The international Jewish community . . . appears to control the big banks, and often the governments; and certainly the mass media."

And who could forget that lovely observation by the French ambassador to Great Britain, at a dinner party in London, about "that shitty little country Israel."

As I say, reasonable debate over Israeli policies is absolutely legitimate. But what should we make of this kind of language? Yes, I know, they're talking about Israelis, not specifically about Jews (though sometimes they do that, too). But when the line is so thin—when Israel has become "the collective Jew"—calling Israelis Nazis opens the speakers up to serious questions about their real motives, no matter how complex the issue.

What's new about the old hatred of Jews, according to Phyllis Chesler, a liberal college professor who has written a book called *The New Anti-Semitism*, "is that [it] has, incredibly been embraced and romanticized by Western liberals, public intellectuals, Nobel

Prize winners and all manner of so-called progressives and activists and, to a great extent, by the presumably objective media. The educated elites claim that they do not in fact hate Jews. How can they—the noblest among the 'politically correct'—be racists? They loathe racism—except, of course, where Jews are concerned."

This assortment of leftists, she says, "have one standard for Israel: an impossibly high one. Meanwhile, they set a much lower standard for every other country, even for nations in which tyranny, torture, honor killings, genocide, and every other human rights abuse go unchallenged."

"Today," she says, "anti-Zionism is the new anti-Semitism."

Can you imagine if Mel Gibson, instead of saying "the Jews are responsible for all the wars in the world," had substituted "Israelis" for "Jews"? A simple, one-word edit in his drunken tirade and he "would have [been] a darling of right-thinking progressives the world over," as Bret Stephens put it in the *Wall Street Journal*.

So the irony of all ironies is that the intellectual "progressive" Left has made Jew-bashing not only palatable but, in some very respectable places, downright acceptable. Thanks to left-wing intellectuals, anti-Semitism is no longer the sole domain of the right-wing fringe. At least the two extremes can unite over something.

Iraq has a lot to do with the new anti-Semitism. Liberals hate George Bush so much that the hard-core among them are willing to believe that American-Jewish support for Israel—the "Jew among nations"—is behind what they see as the whole misbegotten mess. If it weren't for the Jewish lobby that they believe controls the news media and just about everything in America, the dreaded neo-cons (some of whom are Jewish, you see) would not have beat the drums and gotten us into such a bloody quagmire with no end in sight. Or so the argument goes.

This, by the way, seems to be precisely the argument put forth by two prominent conservatives in the media—Robert Novak and

Pat Buchanan. Novak has never had a good word to say about the Israelis. Brutal oppression in other parts of the world rarely interests him. But if an Israeli looks cross-eyed at a Palestinian, Novak sees a crime against humanity. As for Pat Buchanan, he once called Capitol Hill "Israeli-occupied territory." And right before the first Gulf War, he went on the *McLaughlin Group* TV show to announce that "There are only two groups that are beating the drums for war in the Middle East—the Israeli defense ministry and its amen corner in the United States."

You'll forgive me if I wonder if these two paleoconservatives, who opposed the Iraq war from the outset (as did I, by the way), are merely anti-Israel or something a tad more sinister, like anti-Semitic. The line, after all, can be pretty blurry.

As for liberal intellectuals, they think that because they're well educated and supposedly enlightened, then *by definition* they can't possibly be bigots. And that's what makes them so dangerous. They hold important positions at important universities, and because of that they have the power to make bigotry (at least seem) more legitimate. If it's coming from some goober in overalls, that's one thing. If it's coming from a professor at a prestigious university, well, that's something else entirely.

Even a goober who can spot a bad Jew a mile away can figure that out.

Never Mind

Forget every word you just read. Ignore it all.
Sorry.

I have just visited Arianna Huffington's Web site, the much-ballyhooed Huffington Post—and my head is still spinning from what I read there. Here's the scoop: There is no such thing as liberal anti-Semitism. It's physically impossible.

I'm not kidding. But that's not the big news. This is: It's all a conservative plot! That's right, it's a conspiracy to make liberals look bad.

The piece that lays this all out was written by a fellow named Sheldon Drobny, who must be taken seriously because he is the co-founder of Air America Radio. It seems that Mr. Drobny noticed how vicious liberals on the Web could be when the subject gets around to Israel. For a while, this troubled him. How could his fellow liberals possibly be bigots? Then he figured it out. They're not. They're victims . . . of . . . guess who? Here's Drobny's bombshell:

"So my conclusion is that the bloggers who violently hate Israel and see it in black and white terms are not really liberals. They may even be anti-Semites, but they are not representative of the liberal community that was so active in achieving racial and ethnic equality. It is a contradiction for a true liberal to be an anti-Semite. Furthermore, I would not put it past the right wing to flood the liberal blogs with hateful criticisms of Israel to advance a perception that liberals are anti-Israel or anti-Semitic. And I see Karl Rove's finger-prints all over this."

Yes! Exactly! It's the right wing and their evil mastermind Karl Rove, who are behind it all. How could I have missed it? Maybe Karl Rove took control of my mind and didn't tell me.

★ ★ ★ ★ ★ ★ ★ ★ ★ ★ ★

Donkeys to the Left of Me ... Pigs to the Right

His Brother
Was Worse

There's an old joke about a minister conducting a funeral service, who requests that members of his congregation come up and say a few nice words about the deceased—a man widely known to have been a miserable human being. No one goes up. So the minister tries again, "Will someone *please* come up and say something nice about our dearly departed?" Again, no one moves. Now the minister is desperate. "Surely there must be at least *one* person in church today who will say a few kind words as a final good-bye." A man way in the back row gets up and shouts, "His brother was worse!"

When it comes to federal spending, that's how a lot of us feel about the Democrats in Washington. They're worse. But that's not saying much these days.

Democrats may howl about how the federal budget is dripping in red ink, but that doesn't mean they cut spending now that they're in control of Congress. In fact, there's a better chance that Britney Spears will decide to get out of show business, enroll at MIT, and study nuclear physics under the tutelage of Professor Paris Hilton than there is that Democrats will cut even two cents out of the next federal budget. But there is one important difference between Democrats and Republicans. Republicans like to spend like crazy *but* not raise taxes. Democrats like to spend like crazy *and* raise taxes. Why do I keep thinking of that Jim Carrey movie, *Dumb and Dumber*?

But this isn't about Democrats. They took over in 2007. This is about the other miserable brother—the Republicans. After George W. Bush became president, the party of small government spent money like Imelda Marcos in a shoe store. At least Ms. Marcos never pretended to be financially responsible.

Nothing infuriates fiscal conservatives more than out-of-control federal spending. Not immigration (an issue that divides conservatives), not affirmative action (an issue Republicans are too afraid to talk about), not even gay marriage (which is important mainly to religious conservatives). Limited-government conservatives see all this spending as an abandonment of conservative principles, which of course it is. And they feel betrayed. Republicans are supposed to be the grown-ups, the sensible ones, the ones who care about fiscal responsibility and all that. Once upon a time, Republicans were the ones who thought tax money should pay for defense on the national level and cops and garbage pickup on the local level. And that pretty much was that.

In 2005, the libertarian Cato Institute issued a report called "Grand Old Spending Party," which says, "When a Republican-controlled Congress was facing the big-spending tendencies of a Democratic White House, they were more apt to fight to keep spending under control. When Republicans took control of both ends of Pennsylvania Avenue, however, the story changed." The party that used to blast Democrats for spending our "hard-earned money" on every social welfare boondoggle under the sun started doing exactly the same thing. You take over both houses of Congress *and* the White House and you get drunk on the power. You forget what you stand for. Republicans shamelessly became the *defenders* of big government.

How bad is it? According to the Cato Institute's report, "President Bush has presided over the largest overall increase in inflation-adjusted federal spending since Lyndon B. Johnson. Even excluding spending on defense and homeland security, Bush is still the biggest-spending president in 30 years."

Some specifics:

★ Federal spending has grown twice as fast under President Bush as under President Bill Clinton; 65 percent of it unrelated to national security.

★ Spending on education has more than doubled since President Bush took office in 2001.

★ In 2001, President Bush and the Republican Congress spent $286 billion on thirty-three anti-poverty programs. By 2005, the amount spent had grown to $397 billion—a 39-percent increase while inflation went up only 10 percent.

"The GOP was once effective at controlling non-defense spending," the Cato report says. "The final non-defense budgets under Clinton were a combined $57 billion *smaller* than what he proposed from 1996 to 2001. Under Bush, Congress passed budgets that spent a total of $91 billion *more* than the president requested for domestic programs." [Emphasis added.]

You'd think this might bother a supposedly conservative president. Well, if it has, it hasn't bothered him all that much. He didn't veto a single spending bill—not while the Republicans were in office anyway—*not one*!

What is so aggravating about the Republican sellout is that they actually thought they could beat the Democrats at their own game. They decided to build their political base by throwing money at all sorts of constituencies. They spent billions on prescription drugs for seniors and billions more for farmers and then there were the billions for school kids, which they figured wouldn't hurt with those soccer moms in the suburbs, the ones who see themselves as moderates and can go either way in a national election. You know that old Everett Dirksen line: A billion here, a billion there, and pretty soon you're talking about real money.

Over the years, presidents of both parties have had to make tough decisions during difficult times. Roosevelt cut domestic spending during World War II by nearly 40 percent, and Truman, who presided over the Korean War, cut it by about 30 percent—in just one year. As the Cato report says, "Throughout the past 40 years, most presidents have cut or restrained lower-priority spending to make room for higher-priority spending. What is driving George W. Bush's budget is a reversal of that trend."

While they were in power, Republicans spent like there was no tomorrow. And for a lot of them, after the midterm election in 2006, there was no tomorrow. But that could be just the beginning of their troubles. If they don't once again become the party of fiscal responsibility, small-government conservatives will have plenty of reasons to drift away. They just might stay home on Election Day 2008 or they might even find some other party more hospitable to their thinking. Crazier things have happened. It may be true that Democrats are worse. But that won't be enough to save Republican big spenders from themselves.

The Princes
of Pork

In 1987, Ronald Reagan vetoed a highway bill because it included 121 pork projects and was $10 billion over the line he said he would not cross. "I haven't seen this much lard since I handed out blue ribbons at the Iowa State Fair," Reagan said at the time.

And after he was elected president, George W. Bush picked up where Reagan left off. He did what fiscal conservatives do: He declared war on frivolous government spending. In his State of the Union address in 2004 he called on Congress "to cut wasteful spending, and be wise with the people's money." But just one year later, the war was over. Bush had surrendered.

Congress had sent him a $286 billion dollar transportation bill, money that was supposed to go for road building and public transit systems to ease congestion on our highways. But the bill contained all sorts of goodies that had nothing to do with traffic. In fact, it contained a record 6,371 pet projects inserted by members of Congress from both parties—including $6 million to clean up graffiti in New York; nearly $4 million for the National Packard Museum in Warren, Ohio, and the Henry Ford Museum in Dearborn, Michigan; $2.3 million for the beautification of the Ronald Reagan Freeway in California; $2.4 million for the Red River National Wildlife Visitor Center in Louisiana; and $1.2 million for lighting, steps, and equipment at the Blue Ridge Music Center in Virginia.

Taxpayer organizations begged President Bush to veto the bill. But he wouldn't do it. By way of explanation, a White House spokesman simply said, "The president has to work with the Congress," as if collusion in defense of pork were some kind of virtue. Abandoning their fiscal discipline is one of the reasons the Republicans lost control of both the House and the Senate in 2006.

★

There's an old line about how politicians are like diapers. They both need to be changed, a lot, and for the same reason. This, of course, is unfair. Diapers serve a useful purpose.

By and large, the kind of people who go into politics are precisely the kind of people we should discourage from going into politics. This is not to say that there aren't a few profiles in courage in Washington. But more often than not politicians are made of the wrong stuff. They're too eager to please too many constituencies. People with courage usually do other things.

It takes courage, for example, for a politician to tell the folks back home, "No, we're not going to spend money on pork, not when we need every penny to fight the war on terrorism. Not when we have troops fighting in Iraq and Afghanistan." That means no federal money for car museums in Warren, Ohio. No money to clean up graffiti in the Bronx. No money for bridges to nowhere in Alaska, either.

Spend it instead on more security at our airports, our train stations, our ports, our nuclear power plants. Spend it on bigger salaries for our soldiers. Spend it on better equipment for them, too. But don't spend a cent on nonessential pet projects that don't serve the national purpose. Not during wartime. It's unpatriotic.

Easier said than done.

★

Years ago, when I was a correspondent on the CBS News program *48 Hours*, we used to go out all the time to do stories about junkies. I saw these people up close and personal. I saw them shoot heroin in alleyways. I saw them walk around like zombies after they smoked crack. And you know what? Money in the hands of Washington politicians is like crack or heroin in the hands of a drug addict. No difference, as far as I'm concerned. They're both hooked; they're both weak, they both like the high their addiction provides, and neither of them really wants to kick the habit. And nowhere is this pathology more evident than when it comes to something the insiders in Washington call "earmarks."

"Earmarks" is an insipid, nondescript term that sounds harmless and means absolutely nothing to most Americans, who know the term by its more familiar name: *pork*. We learned all about pork in junior high civics class. Politicians love to "bring home the bacon," so somebody came up with a one-word way to describe it. *Pork* is not a bad word, but I prefer another: *bribery*.

This kind, unfortunately, is legal. But it's bribery, nonetheless. Here's how it works: Members of Congress, who too often are nothing more than glorified errand boys and girls, get a call from some local political hack back in the home district, who says, "You know, we sure could use some money for that tomato museum we've been wanting to build. Sure would put a lot of folks to work. Yes sir. And it would bring in lots of tourists. The shop owners in town sure would be mighty grateful. So would the contractors who would build the museum, if you know what I mean."

Translation: "If you get us *free* Washington money, we won't have to pay for the museum with local tax money. Then, some of those grateful contractors will kick back—oops, sorry—will *contribute* money to your reelection campaign, which you could use to run TV and newspaper ads reminding voters that you're the one who got them the *free* money for their tomato museum."

Like I said, it's bribery—bribery made easy because "earmarks" traditionally have sailed through the system under the radar, often without hearings and just before the clock strikes midnight. In fact, lawmakers didn't even have to put their names on their pet pork projects. They just attached them to important pieces of legislation that had absolutely nothing to do with tomato museums or graffiti. This raises an important question: How can any decent American who works hard and pays taxes not detest these gutless wonders?

Both parties, of course, love to buy votes with pork. And rest assured, despite any so-called "reforms" imposed by the new Democratically controlled Congress—*pork is not going away!* If these politicians were running a private corporation and tried anything like that, they'd spend the next ten years in prison. In Washington, where tax money is everybody's money, and everybody's money has a way of becoming nobody's money, it's called business as usual. As P. J. O'Rourke once said, "Giving a politician power and money is like giving a teenage boy a car and alcohol."

But Democrats never pretended to be for small government. They tell you right up front that they're going to spend your money like drunken sailors; and from time to time, when they get careless, they'll even admit that they'll raise your taxes to pay for it all. Walter Mondale tried that in 1984. It didn't work. Reagan won 59 percent of the vote and carried forty-nine states.

Republicans, on the other hand, brag about how they're the party of fiscal responsibility, which used to be true. No more. Which is one of the reasons they're now the minority party in Washington.

It was a Republican big spender, you may recall—Senator Ted Stevens of Alaska, *who just happened to be head of the Senate Appropriations Committee*—who led the fight for that $223 million

"Bridge to Nowhere"—a bridge that would have connected Ketchikan, Alaska, to an island populated by about fifty people. The very idea of such a bridge was so embarrassing (even by Washington standards) that it died a slow death in Congress, which prompted Senator Stevens to thunder on the floor of the Senate: "I will resign from this body." He didn't, of course.

There's also a bridge near Anchorage, which you're paying for, a bridge called "Don Young's Way." Who, you naively ask, is Don Young? Well, he's the Republican congressman from Alaska, who used his considerable influence *as chairman of the Transportation Committee*, to get the money for the bridge in the first place.

Here are some other statistics that should prove that shame, like courage, is in short supply in Washington.

Since 1991, federal spending on pork projects has increased by 900 percent. Has your salary gone up that much? How about the stock market? How about *anything* else?

In 2005 and 2006, Congress added a total of 23,960 earmarks to its spending bills costing taxpayers $56 billion. According to the public watchdog group Citizens Against Government Waste, Congress porked over $13.5 million to the International Fund for Ireland, which helped finance the World Toilet Summit; $1 million for the Water-free Urinal Conservation Initiative; $1.3 million for berry research in Alaska; and $500,000 for the Sparta Teapot Museum in Sparta, North Carolina—to name just a few random projects America couldn't do without.

Since 1985, Congress has spent 86 million taxpayer dollars for "wood utilization research." It spent another $65.7 million for shrimp aquaculture research. According to the U.S. Department of Agriculture, "The goal of this program is to develop a sustainable domestic shrimp-farming industry in the United States." According to Citizens Against Government Waste, "The timeline for this program appears to be indefinite."

In its 2006 "Pig Book Summary," Citizens Against Government Waste says, "The guilty pleas of lobbyist Jack Abramoff and former Rep. Randy 'Duke' Cunningham illustrate how pork-barrel projects, whether used as currency for re-election or as political favors to well-connected individuals or businesses, can corrupt the political process. The historic lack of restraint in the appropriations process has helped create a projected $371 billion budget deficit in fiscal 2006 and a national debt of $8.5 trillion. Whether the lobbying scandal and the outrage of taxpayers over 'bridges to nowhere' will force Congress to cut the pork remains to be seen."

Yes it does. But we're already getting a glimpse of the future—and I'm afraid it looks an awful lot like the past. In January 2007, the new Republican minority leaders in the House decided to teach one of their own a lesson: They kicked Jeff Flake, a no-nonsense fiscal conservative from Arizona, off the Judiciary Committee, his most important congressional assignment. His crime? Trying to kill billions in wasteful pork projects—and having the nerve to go on *60 Minutes* to tell America just how bad it is up there on Capitol Hill. If the Republican leadership had any brains, they would have given Flake a medal for his courage. Instead they punished him, proving that Republicans learned nothing from the drubbing they took on Election Day 2006. This is a party that is losing its soul, and you get the impression they don't even know it.

So, given their arrogance, do Republicans, and other politicians, have what it takes to clean up their act? Anything is possible, I guess. Even junkies have been known to kick the habit. But should we really expect the same strength of character from politicians with trillions of other people's money to spend? Frankly, I don't think so. In fact, there's an old joke that pretty much sums up the character of these "profiles in courage" and the "high esteem" in which they're held:

"Don't tell my mother I'm in politics. She thinks I play the piano in a whorehouse."

Extreme Makeover: Republican Edition

Here are a few tips from me to the stupid Republicans who thought it was smart politics to outspend the Democrats:

Rule #1: You can never outspend Democrats. Never. It is mathematically impossible. Like trying to reach infinity, it cannot be done.

Rule #2: You can never out-compassion Democrats. They own the issue.

Rule #3: No matter how much money Republicans throw at the voters in an attempt to make over their image, it will never be enough. They can never shed their mean-spirited, we-don't-give-a-damn-about-the-poor label. The liberal media simply won't let it happen.

If you need proof that Republicans can never do enough, consider these examples:

During a budget debate in Washington, when the Republicans were still in charge, the American Federation of State, County and Municipal Employees union ran a television ad that said: "The Republican House just voted to slash health care for struggling families, cut college loans for middle-class kids, and take food off the tables of poor children."

New York Democratic Congressman Charles Rangel threw his two cents in, telling the *Washington Post,* "I don't know what the poor, the elderly, the disabled, or our foster children have done to Republicans to deserve this."

During the last presidential election, liberals came up with a bumper sticker that portrayed George Bush as a monster feeding on poor people: BUSH '04—EAT THE POOR.

Facts mean nothing to liberals when it comes to government spending. But here are a few anyway:

- ★ According to the Heritage Foundation, in 2004, 16.3 percent of the federal budget went to antipoverty programs. This is the highest it's ever been.
- ★ Between 2001 and 2005, President Bush and those cold-hearted Republicans in Congress increased spending on antipoverty programs by $111 billion.
- ★ Between 2001 and 2005, the aforementioned Republican cheapskates increased housing aid by 26 percent; cash assistance to the poor by 37 percent; health care by 40 percent; and food support by 49 percent.

Which brings us to:

Rule #4: Republicans who try to repeal rules #1, 2, and/or 3 above will succeed only in losing an important constituency—fiscal conservatives, who will instantly see the cynical game they're playing and despise them for it. They saw it in 2006, didn't they?

★ ★ ★ ★ ★ ★ ★ ★ ★ ★ ★

Islam Is a Religion of Peace, and If You Don't Believe Me I'll Kill You

Profiles in Foolishness

I don't know about you, but I started feeling a lot safer as soon as those security guards at the airport began taking shampoo away from old ladies and toothpaste away from little kids. Before that I used to be afraid to fly. Now I'm breathing a whole lot easier. Phew, thank God the masterminds who are looking out for our safety figured out a way to foil the terrorists!

But the no-shampoo/no-toothpaste rules didn't last long. Now they tell us we *can* take toothpaste and shampoo on board the plane—but only if the tube or bottle contains no more than three ounces of the deadly stuff *and* is packed in a clear, one-quart-size baggie. If your three ounces of toothpaste is packed in a *two*-quart baggie, they won't let you on the plane with it. That would be way too dangerous. Nor will they let you on with *four* ounces of shampoo in a one-quart clear baggie. How about if you have just two ounces of aftershave lotion left sitting in a five-ounce bottle? Sorry. Strictly against the rules!

You may recall that these regulations went into effect ten minutes after Scotland Yard caught those Muslims in London who the Brits said were trying to blow up airplanes in the sky by mixing liquids once on board. I have it on good authority that the guys from Monty Python came up with these rules in response.

I could put up with this nonsense if the TSA people at the airport weren't so damn evenhanded. I could handle it a lot better if they didn't target everybody *equally*; because each person going through security at the airport simply does not pose the same potential threat. Whether we want to admit it or not, most of us probably agree that a twenty-year-old Muslim man from Saudi Arabia should get a closer look than an eighty-five-year-old Methodist grandmother from Peoria.

But that's not how we do it. Under our current idiotic rules, Grandma gets the same going-over as the young Muslim. This would make sense, as the Canadian columnist Rachel Marsden has put it, "if the Golden Girls were blowing up planes." Since they're not, this kind of mindless "equality" is not just dumb. It's dangerous.

It's time to stop the PC lunacy. We need ethnic profiling at our airports. Whether it's checking the luggage of Arab passengers more closely or asking them to step out of line for a few probing questions about where they've been and where they're going, we need to scrutinize young Arab men more closely than everybody else. Sorry if that's not PC. But we need to do it. And we need to do it now.

You'd have to be deaf, dumb, and blind—or work for the government—to not have noticed that the terrorists have certain traits in common. They're Muslims. They're Arabs. They're almost always young men.

No, that doesn't mean security agents should grab every young Arab Muslim man in line and strip-search the guy. Obviously not all young Muslim men from the Middle East are jihadists.

But the current PC airport regulations are destructive. They breed disrespect for authority. Am I really supposed to take some guy with a badge seriously when he's taking a bottle of Prell and tube of Crest away from some old lady? I understand that the TSA guys are just following orders, but they remind me of a bunch of Barney Fife wannabes—Andy Taylor's deputy sheriff in Mayberry who liked to play tough with those dangerous criminals who didn't put enough money in the parking meter.

★

We need new rules. Smart ones. Un-PC rules. We need to understand that profiling is a small price to pay for living in a free country at a time when terrorists are out to kill us. It was, after all, *Muslims* who attacked us—not Eskimos, not Chinese, not Aborigines from Australia, and not old ladies from the American Midwest!

So yes, the security agents at the airport should treat young Arab men differently than they treat everybody else. The civil liberty I care most about in a post–9/11 world is that of my ass not getting blown up by one of these lunatics!

But what about converts to radical Islam—men and women who don't fit the profile? And what about Timothy McVeigh, the white man who blew up the federal building in Oklahoma City? He wasn't a Muslim, the critics of profiling keep reminding us. This is a fair point, but it is hardly an argument against ethnic profiling. Let's keep an eye on all sorts of people at the airport. But let's also play the odds. Let's focus on the people most likely to try to do us harm—young Arab men.

★

When then–transportation secretary Norman Mineta went on *60 Minutes* three weeks after 9/11, my old CBS News colleague Steve Kroft asked him if a seventy-year-old white woman from Vero Beach, Florida, should receive the same kind of scrutiny as a Muslim man from Jersey City. Mineta said, "Basically, I would hope so." Could he imagine any set of circumstances, Kroft asked, "that would justify ethnic and racial profiling at our airports?" "Absolutely not," came the reply.

Mineta should have been fired before the show went off the air. But who was going to do the firing? George W. Bush? He's too busy spouting homilies about how Islam is "a religion of peace," a point that must make all those Muslim terrorists who take their marching orders from Allah chuckle in disbelief.

The problem with Norman Mineta was that he was a captive of history. His own, unfortunately. After the attack on Pearl Harbor, Mineta, his family, and anyone else who was Japanese-American were thrown into internment camps by the United States government. Their rights were clearly violated, even if the United States Supreme Court didn't think so at the time. So who better to stand foursquare against ethnic profiling? Challenge Mineta, in our liberal PC culture, and you run the risk of being called a bigot, someone who's in favor of rounding up Arab-Americans and throwing them all into modern-day concentration camps.

What America did to Japanese-Americans during World War II was beyond disgraceful. It remains a stain on our nation's history. But it is not in the same moral galaxy as profiling, as simply scrutinizing more closely Arab males of a certain age, since Arab males of a certain age are the ones most likely to try to blow up airplanes.

Everybody, including Floyd Abrams, the distinguished constitutional lawyer and champion of individual rights, knows this to be true. On that same *60 Minutes* program, Abrams said, "There's a big difference between being interned and being searched a little more at an airport. . . . Right now, we're in an emergency situation, we've been attacked, and the one thing that the attackers have in common so far is their national origin and their sex and their language. And for us to say, 'Well, you know, we just can't think about that, we'll just put that aside, because, call it political correctness, call it anything, we just won't think about it because it makes us feel uncomfortable,' is an appalling malfeasance."

"The law does some foolish things; it doesn't do crazy things," Abrams said. "It would be crazy not to consider what people look like when we're looking for people who may be involved with hijacking."

In 2006—five years too late, as far as I'm concerned—Norman Mineta resigned as transportation secretary. But, of course, his departure changed absolutely nothing as far as ethnic profiling at our airports is concerned. The compassionate-conservative Bush administration remains opposed to it.

So do the Democrats, who think it's a good idea to take ethnicity and gender into account—in other words, to profile—when it's time to decide who gets into college or who gets a government job, but think it's a bad idea to take ethnicity and gender into account when we're trying to spot potential terrorists at the airport. Let's see if I have this right: The only time we're supposed to be against profiling is when our national security is on the line?

Paging Barney Fife.

★

I'm watching the news late at night, about the Muslims arrested in London, when the phone rings. It's almost midnight, and it's a friend calling from California—a friend who never heard of the three-hour time difference.

"Here's my idea for what we should do at airports," he tells me. "Two lines: One only for Arabs and the other for everyone else."

"Are you nuts," I yell at him. *"You can't do that."*

"And you know what else we need?" he asks as if he didn't hear what I just said. "We need a new airline. AFA."

I know I'm asking for trouble, but I ask anyway, very slowly. "What does AFA stand for?"

"Arab Free Airlines," he says without a hint of humor. "I tried this on my liberal friends here in California," he tells me, "and they were appalled. *Appalled!* Then I asked them: You all have kids, right? Would you rather fly AFA with your kids or some other airline? Every one of them said, AFA."

"Dumbo," I say, "this is insane. You can't have an airline that doesn't let Arabs on board. That's number one. Number two, regarding your two lines at the airport idea, one for Arabs, the other for everybody else: As soon as we profile young Arab men, the terrorists will hand their bombs off to tall, blond Swedish women."

"Fine," he says, without missing a beat. "Then, while we're standing in those long lines to get through the security checkpoint, we can all watch the TSA people strip-search *them*. That'll make the airport experience a little easier to take."

My friend isn't crazy, but I can't swear to that. He knows that what he has just said is sure to offend all sorts of people. But like a lot of us, he's disgusted with all the problems a relatively few radical Muslims are causing in the world—and he doesn't think taking shampoo away from Grandma and cinnamon-sparkle toothpaste from little Billy is the solution. Neither does Republican congressman Peter King.

After the London plot was foiled, King went on TV and said: "We need to have a lot more common sense. If the IRA had blown up Lower Manhattan, then people with Irish names and red hair and freckles should be stopped more than an African-American or an Italian-American. It makes no sense frisking eighty-year-old women and allowing others to walk through without being stopped. If you want to call it profiling or more intelligent screening, yes it has to be done and it should be done."

Too bad Peter King is one of only a few Republicans willing to throw political correctness to the wind and speak with clarity in these difficult times. Instead of running away from profiling, President Bush ought to explain to the nation why we need it, why we're all in this war on terror together, and why some people might have to put up with a little inconvenience for the sake of everybody's well-being.

But it'll never happen. So fasten your seat belts; it could be a bumpy ride. Because if we remain the captives of PC rules, and if two or three terrorists sail through security while the TSA guys are going through my aunt Tilly's suitcase to make sure she's not sneaking too much conditioner on the plane, and if God forbid they bring down an airplane, then a whole bunch of people—Democrats, Republicans, and everybody else—are going to think my crazy California friend's ideas—about two lines at the airport, one for Arabs the other for everybody else; and about an Arab Free Airline—aren't that crazy after all.

See No Evil

I'm not a dinner-party kind of guy. I don't do well at them. In fact, I'd rather do hard time in a Saudi Arabian prison than attend a dinner party with people I don't know and whom, after a few minutes of inane small talk, I find pretentious and boring. Besides, I can't eat food that is served on a plate adorned with raspberry drizzle. It makes me feel gay. Not that there's anything wrong with that.

So I'm at just such a dinner party in Miami, and I'm thinking of stabbing myself with the fish knife, when the conversation turns to terrorism and my ears perk up.

People know that I'm a journalist and they want to hear my take on the subject. So I tell them. "Islam is not a religion like most of the others," I say. "It's different, and not in a good way."

Since this is a liberal crowd, the room goes silent. People don't talk this way in polite company. Liberals have convinced themselves that all religions and all cultures are of equal value—except maybe Christianity and the United States, which many of them see as less than equal.

Knowing how uncomfortable I'm making everybody, I feel invigorated.

"Jews don't blow things up when they get angry," I continue. "They don't say, 'We're a religion of peace and if you don't believe us we'll kill you.' Christians don't cut people's heads off because they don't like what they just said. Hindus don't try to kill cartoonists because they made fun of Hindus. Muslims are different."

And they are. We all know about the radical Muslims, but too many "good Muslims" just sit there silently while the radicals commit horrendous acts of violence, and then say that while they may not actually condone the violence, they understand it. Muslim solidarity is a very scary and very illiberal concept, one unfortunately lost on a lot of liberals. "These radical Muslims," I tell the room, "need to be crushed. It's really that simple."

Not to a woman sitting two seats to my right it isn't. "We need to understand what motivates them," she tells me and everyone else at the table. "We need to understand the *root causes* of such behavior." She then goes on about how oppression and despair lead to the kind of violence they commit.

I tell her she's wrong. I remind her that most of the terrorists who killed three thousand of our fellow Americans on September 11, 2001, came from the Saudi middle class. I remind her that Osama bin Laden was hardly oppressed growing up; that his family was loaded. And besides, more than a few studies have shown that the most radical Muslims are better educated and have more economic opportunities than the average man on the Arab Street.

Since the woman I'm speaking to is black, I try an analogy that I hope might resonate with her. Does she think, I ask, that back in the 1950s decent Americans should have tried to *understand* what motivated white bigots to lynch black people in the Old South? Did we need to understand the *root causes* that led them to such violence? "You know, there *were* root causes," I tell her. "These white guys felt oppressed and frightened by the rapid changes that were being forced on them. Did we really need to explore that," I ask, "or did we simply need to let them know that while they were free to think whatever they wanted about black people, they were not free to commit violence?"

Before she could answer, I said: "I don't care what motivated those bigots. What they did was wrong. It was criminal. Period."

I knew I was wasting my time, mainly because I figured out some time ago that while liberals rightly detest homegrown terrorists—Timothy McVeigh comes to mind—they're more *open-minded* about the international variety, and frankly, are more than willing to see America as the bad guy, as a stand-in for all Western sin against so-called oppressed peoples. Never mind that these poor *oppressed* radical Muslims believe that strapping bombs on their bodies and dying for their religious beliefs is a noble act; that many wanted to kill the pope because he said something that offended them; or that they have no qualms about murdering their own fellow Muslims for the high crime of losing faith in Islam. And liberals think we need to change *our* behavior?

Well, yes. In fact, that's exactly what Andy Rooney, the senior resident liberal at *60 Minutes* thinks. On the fifth anniversary of the 9/11 attacks, Andy shared this little gem with his audience: "Americans are puzzled over why so many people in the world hate us. We seem so nice to ourselves. They do hate us, though. We know that and we're trying to protect ourselves with more weapons. We have to do it I suppose, but it might be better if we figured out how to behave as a nation in a way that wouldn't make so many people in the world want to kill us."

Have you ever noticed how *Rooney* rhymes with *loony*?

This is modern-day Democratic liberalism at its most despicable. *If only we behaved differently, then they wouldn't want to kill us.* Would Andy Rooney have ever told black people in Mississippi in 1955: "Yes, white people hate you. But if you would only behave differently, maybe they wouldn't want to lynch you."

Liberals like Andy Rooney can spot America's shortcomings a mile away, but they refuse to see Islamic evil even when it's staring them right in the face. As Sam Harris, an author who has written extensively on religion—and a self-described proud liberal—put it in a piece for the *Los Angeles Times* titled "Head-in-the-Sand Liberals": "The truth is that there is every reason to believe that a terrifying number of the world's Muslims now view all political and moral questions in terms of their affiliation with Islam. This leads them to rally to the cause of other Muslims no matter how sociopathic their behavior. This benighted religious solidarity may be the greatest problem facing civilization and yet is regularly misconstrued, ignored or obfuscated by liberals."

This is why liberalism in America is becoming increasingly irrelevant. Liberals have lost touch with reality.

★

On Rush Limbaugh's radio show, on September 11, 2006, a liberal caller said the attack on America five years earlier was "an inside job." Most liberals, of course, are not so deranged. But a surprising number are. Start with a group of liberal college professors who call themselves "Scholars for 9/11 Truth." They teach at major American colleges, like the University of Minnesota and Wisconsin and New Hampshire, to name just a few. And they believe the very same thing as that caller to Rush's radio show: that the United States attacked itself on September 11, 2001, as part of a giant White House conspiracy to smooth the way for war in Iraq, Afghanistan, and who knows where else.

There's more. According to a poll by the Scripps Survey Research Center, more than a third of Americans think the U.S. government "assisted in the 9/11 terrorist attacks or took no action to stop them so the United States could go to war in the Middle East." Sixteen percent believe the twin towers of the World Trade Center came down not because jet planes loaded with fuel flew into them but because agents of the Bush administration blew them up.

"Such an astonishing eruption of masochistic unreason could

well mark the decline of liberalism, if not the decline of Western civilization," as Sam Harris—who, remember, is a liberal himself—put it.

Yes, the "inside job" crowd represents only a subset of liberalism. But lots of liberals who consider themselves mainstream believe all sorts of other crazy things: that our government is run by fascists and other criminals who would lie, cheat, and steal to enrich their friends at Halliburton, for example. If you think that, how big a leap is it to believe that we attacked ourselves on 9/11 to protect our oil interests in the Middle East?

It's fascinating, and not in a good way, that so many liberals who cavalierly throw the word *fascism* around to describe people in the Bush administration are blind to the real thing. They don't see Muslim terrorists as fascists, but like my dinner-party companion, they see them as those oppressed people who need our understanding. This may make liberals feel good about themselves, but all they're doing with their "compassion" is smothering the life right out of American liberalism.

So don't blame Rush Limbaugh if fewer and fewer Americans take liberalism seriously. This is not the doing of conservatives. Liberals are committing suicide. Put the blame where it belongs. On Andy Rooney, and all the other "head-in-the-sand liberals."

What's Round, Lisps, Cracks Jokes, and Kills Jews?

Once again, the *New York Times* has ruined what would otherwise have been a perfectly good day.

It always starts the same way. I always make the same dumb mistake. *I open the paper.* Will I never learn?

On this day, in a hotel room in Los Angeles, I'm reading a news story about the leader of Hezbollah, Sheikh Hassan Nasrallah. Actually, "news story" isn't quite the right term. "Lap dance" is more like it.

Sheikh Nasrallah is a religious leader *and* a military commander, both at the same time, which means that when he is not praying to Allah he is ordering his men to fire rockets into Israeli cities with the express purpose of killing civilians. This, by definition, makes him a terrorist. But "terrorist" is a word that never appears in this story about the sheikh.

Instead, we're told that "He comes across as far less dour than most Shiite clerics partly due to his roly-poly figure and slight lisp." We're also told that he "cracks jokes."

The main thrust of the piece is that Nasrallah is "a new icon" in the Arab world, mainly because unlike previous Arab leaders, who only talked tough, the sheikh has put some real muscle behind his rhetoric. "Gone are the empty threats made by President Gamal Abdel Nasser's official radio station during the 1967 Arab-Israeli war to push the Jews into the sea even as Israel seized Jerusalem,

163

the Golan Heights and the Sinai Peninsula," the *Times* story says.

"Gone is Saddam Hussein's idle vow to 'burn half of Israel,' only to launch limited volleys of sputtering scuds."

Instead, the Arab world now has a real man, the story says, "a 46-year-old Lebanese militia chieftain hiding in a bunker, combining the scripted logic of a clergyman with the steely resolve of a general to completely re-write the Arab-Israeli land feud."

He knows his audience so well, we're told, that some say he has the "Disney touch."

The Disney touch? This whole story is Goofy, I'm thinking. My day is shot. The *Times* is actually portraying this religious bigot as a "roly-poly" guy "with a slight lisp," who likes to "crack jokes." Am I reading the *Times* or *People* magazine? It can't get any worse, I mutter to myself. But, of course, I'm wrong. It's just my old friend wishful thinking yanking my chain.

Just a few paragraphs down, I read the following: Sheikh Nasrallah thinks "all Jewish immigrants should return to their countries of origin and that there should be one Palestine with equality for Muslims, Jews and Christians."

So now I'm wondering: Is this just sloppy reporting or is it willful ignorance? Does the veteran Middle East *New York Times* reporter who has written this valentine—Neil MacFarquhar—really believe this nonsense? Is he really unaware of the other things the sheikh has said about Jews? If he had only checked LexisNexis, MacFarquhar (or his editor back in New York) would have found this quotation from the good sheikh that doesn't quite seem to jibe with his more "benevolent" observations about Jews living in peace with Muslims and Christians in "one Palestine":

"If the Jews all gather in Israel, it will save us the trouble of going after them worldwide."

That's not exactly a small omission. Not some irrelevant point. The *Times*, which thinks it's important to tell us that the sheikh and his Party of God run "hospitals, schools and other social services," apparently doesn't think it's important to mention that they also hide rockets and other weapons in the basements of those hospitals and schools—to ensure that civilians will become human shields in times of war.

And, in case you're wondering, no, the quotation about gathering up the world's Jews in Israel isn't some made-up Israeli dirty trick. It comes from an interview the sheikh gave to a major Lebanese newspaper in 2002. In fact, a host on NPR talked about the sheikh and his remark about the Jews on July 18, 2006, just three weeks before the *Times* ran its piece. Here's the verbatim exchange between NPR anchor Alex Chadwick and his guest Fawaz Gerges, a scholar of Middle Eastern studies, who teaches at Sarah Lawrence College:

Chadwick: Here's a quote from a big newspaper in Lebanon, the *Daily Star*. This is from four years ago in an interview with a Hezbollah leader, Sayyed Hassan Nasrallah, the man who's speaking for Hezbollah today. He said then: "If they, the Jews, all gather in Israel, it will save us the trouble of going after them worldwide."

Prof. Gerges: A very disturbing quote. The rhetoric of Nasrallah and his cohorts, very hostile. . . . I think the rhetoric is very volatile. It's very insensitive, and it's very racist.

But you didn't read any of that in the *Times* story. Not a word about Nasrallah's master plan for the destruction of every last Jew in the world. And this is the real problem. Not that MacFarquhar got his facts wrong. But that he decided to leave all sorts of important facts out of his story.

For example, the *Times* dutifully reports that Nasrallah "called the three southern villages where the fiercest clashes erupted 'the triangle of heroism, manhood, courage and gallantry.'" But journalism isn't stenography. We get nothing on just how, in the sheikh's mind, it is heroic, manly, courageous, or gallant to hide among Lebanese civilians, fire rockets into Israel, and then put the lives of his own countrymen in jeopardy when the Israelis respond. The people who have told us about the sheikh's "Disney touch" apparently have nothing to say about this.

The *Times* is always fretting about bigotry and hate speech—apparently, though, not when the offending bigot is the "heroic" leader of a band of guerrillas fighting for his people's honor. In the past, when the *Times* kissed up to such tyrants—Fidel Castro comes to mind—at least it was naive journalism *before the fact*. Castro hadn't yet become a ruthless dictator when the *Times* was singing his praises. But Nasrallah is a known quantity, a man of God who could live in peace with his long-suffering people if only the Jews of the world would do him one small favor: gather in nearby Israel to make their slaughter more convenient.

At the end of the *Times* piece, we hear from a few Arabs who don't like the sheikh, including a secretary who says that Nasrallah "is solely responsible for all the destruction." But this strikes me as no more than a belated nod to balance. Journalism, after all, is often about emphasis, and the emphasis in this piece is all in the sheikh's favor. "He has never pushed hard-line Islamic rules like veils for women in the neighborhoods that Hezbollah controls," the *Times* reports. This, I suppose, shows how progressive he is, an always-popular position at the world's most important newspaper.

Finally, a religious fundamentalist the *New York Times* can embrace.

The "Moderates"
Are a Little Nutty, Too

While it's true that most Muslims are not ter-
rorists, it's also true that most terrorists are Muslims—at least the
ones who want to kill *us*. This is why it's time—long past time,
actually—for a Million Muslim Man March.

Why should American Muslims march if they're not blowing anybody up? Is this guilt by association? No. Muslims should
march not to prove their innocence but to let the terrorists know
that good Muslims will not support them—*or even try to understand them*—simply because they share the same religion. Muslims
should march to isolate the radicals who kill in the name of Islam;
to tell them that they are alone in their dark world; to make sure
the fascists who pray to Allah know that they have no allies here
in America.

I told a friend about my idea and after he stopped laughing,
he said, "If you get a Five Muslim Man March, you're lucky." He
thinks I'm a hopeless optimist.

Call me Pollyanna, but I'm not deterred. I don't just want a million Muslims to march on Washington, I want a million more to
march on London, and a million more on Paris, and on Madrid,
and on Frankfurt, and on Rome, and on Amsterdam, on Brussels,
and on every civilized city on the planet. I want them to march on
Cairo and Amman and Damascus and Riyadh, too.

But I know the odds are against all of it. Europe is filled with appeasers too afraid to open their mouths. And the Arab world is an incubator for pathology, where kids learn how to hate before they get out of kindergarten. While American and British children dream of becoming doctors and scientists, Arab kids—too many of them, anyway—have role models who teach them to become martyrs. But that is precisely why Muslims who live in the modern world, in the civilized world, have to speak up.

I tell my friend that my idea isn't as crazy as it sounds. Something like this has actually worked before—right here in America. In the bad days of the Old South, there really weren't a lot of white people who went out at night looking for black people to lynch or beat up or run off the side of the road. In reality, there were very few terrorists in places like Alabama and Mississippi and Louisiana.

But there were millions of other white folks in those places, who just didn't want to get involved. These were the so-called "moderates"—the ones who would never actually commit violence but just looked the other way.

I was a young guy during the civil rights era, living in New Jersey, and I remember thinking that these moderates were just as bad as all the rest. Where was their courage? How could they look the other way when poor people who had done no one any harm were being beaten, and worse? They were either bigots or cowards, I figured. Either way, I despised them.

I admired the few brave souls who stood up to the bigots, the ones who said, "This is wrong and we want the world to know that just because we're also white, we will never condone it." For their courage, they were called "nigger lovers." But as the federal government moved in to enforce the Civil Rights Act, still more white people cast off their fear (or maybe just their prejudices) and changed their ways, refusing to let the past bury any chance for a better future.

There were holdouts, of course, white people who sent their

kids to "Christian Academies," a thinly veiled name for segregation schools. And there were the diehards who blamed all the troubles "on those Northerners." "We were doing just fine down here," they would say with a straight face, "until those outsiders came in and riled up our Negroes."

But there was no turning back the clock. Too many people who had spent a lifetime tolerating bigotry were tired of being embarrassed, tired of allowing the bigots to define who *all* white people were. And by standing up, one at a time, they performed a miracle unimaginable just a decade or so earlier: *They changed the culture.* It took a while, but more and more, the haters became the minority, and eventually they were isolated.

Are there still some bigots out there, all these years later? Sure. But they're an even bigger embarrassment now than they were back then. And most important, they're not getting away with lynching anybody!

Which brings us back to our modern-day haters, the fascists who hatch their evil plots in dark rooms and bright mosques. The fact is there are too many good, decent, moderate Muslims living right in our midst who, like the good, decent, moderate white folks in the Old South, just don't want to get involved.

Or worse.

I was watching the *O'Reilly Factor* the night British police rounded up the usual suspects, and I heard congressman Peter King, a Republican from Long Island, tell Bill, "I feel strongly that it's incumbent on the Muslim community and [its] leadership to speak out and to cooperate much more with the police and law-enforcement authorities than they are currently."

"How do you know they're not cooperating?" O'Reilly asked.

"I know it from talking to police, I know it from talking to people in the community, I know it from a mosque in my own district [some of whose members] for months after 9/11 were saying that the Jews could have attacked the World Trade Center and it wasn't bin Laden. And these were doctors and professionals who live in homes that would put all of us to shame."

Unfortunately, this is not a single story from a lone congressman about a few well-to-do loony Muslims in his district. The delusions are far more widespread. At the annual convention of the Islamic Society of North America in Chicago, in September 2006, a poll was taken on Muslim-American attitudes toward the United States. The results were not exactly encouraging.

When asked "Is the American government at war with the religion of Islam," 68 percent of the Muslim-Americans said yes.

"Did Muslims hijack planes and fly them into buildings on 9/11?" Only 38 percent said yes; 45 percent said no.

What about America's invasion of Afghanistan right after we were attacked on 9/11? Was it justified? Eighty-one percent of the Muslim-Americans polled said it was not justified.

There were also disturbing responses to questions about whether it was okay for Muslims to use violence against the American military. When asked if "violence by Muslims against the American military overseas [is] acceptable, in retaliation for the American government's actions in the Muslim world," half said no, but 44 percent said yes. And while 69 percent said that violence by Muslims against the American military *in the United States* was not acceptable "in retaliation for the American government's actions in the Muslim world"—nearly one in four—24 percent—said it was acceptable.

It's only a straw poll. Only 307 Muslims took part. And it would be nice to think that these Muslim-Americans represent only a small percentage of Muslims living in this country; that they speak only for the delusional wing of Islam. But I fear that would be wishful thinking. These are the ones, after all, who believe the U.S. government has declared war on their religion, and so many of them have concocted their own ideas about who attacked us on 9/11. And keep this in mind: Everyone who took the poll in Chicago—every one!—*is an American citizen.*

This, my friend tells me, is precisely why he's so cynical—or realistic, as he would put it. The ignorance or hate or paranoia runs too deep. "It's part of the culture," he says. "Peter King is right: Even educated Muslims who live in the suburbs subscribe to this crap." And then he drops the famous Golda Meir quote on me: "There will be no peace in the Middle East until the Arabs love their children more than they hate the Jews."

But hatred ran deep in Mississippi, too, I remind him. And it's no longer the same down there. It's better; a lot better. He's not convinced. Not by a long shot.

Back in the '60s in Mississippi, white people finally figured out that it wasn't good enough anymore to look the other way. Not just because it made them accomplices. But because outside of their little bubble, they weren't trusted. They were outcasts. We associated *all of them* with George Wallace and other bigots.

No one wants to say it out loud, but a lot of Americans (like my friend) don't trust the Muslims in our midst today, either; because except for a few brave ones, they haven't spoken up against their fellow Muslims with anything like a loud, clear, unified voice. More often than not, in the face of Islamic terrorism, the vast majority here in America and around the world have chosen to remain silent, to simply stay out of it—or worse, to share their delusions about how the Jews flew those planes into the World Trade Center. You know there's a deep, deep problem when even the so-called moderates come off as screwballs.

Toward the end of 2006, I stumbled on to a little ray of hope, which came in the form of a guest column in the *New York Post*. It was written by an Arab-American named Emilio Karim Dabul, who lives in New Jersey. He used to be afraid to speak out against his fellow Muslims, he wrote, but no more.

"The only time I raised my voice in protest against these men who killed thousands of innocents in the name of Allah [on 9/11] was behind closed doors, among the safety of friends and family," he wrote. But now, he went on, "I'm sick of saying the truth only in private—that Arabs around the world, including Arab-Americans like myself, need to start holding our own culture accountable for the insane, violent actions that our extremists have perpetrated on the world at large."

This is a start, I tell my friend. This can be the beginning of a new day when decent people can shed their fears and their prejudices and finally start to separate themselves in a very real way from the violent bad guys. After a short pause, I ask him: "Still think I'm a hopeless optimist?"

"Yes, I do," he tells me almost before I get the question out of my mouth.

I fear he's right. But I pray he's wrong.

Good Television

I'm in Los Angeles, and I wake up to the pictures of those children with blue faces, their mouths packed with dirt. The reporters are saying that Israeli rockets have hit an apartment building in a Lebanese village called Qana and that many civilians—more than fifty, they think—have been killed; half of them children, the youngest only ten months old.

Tragedy always plays well on television. Especially when children are involved. And these pictures are certainly heartbreaking; they make you want to change the channel.

But of course you don't. Because in the perverse world of broadcasting, death, destruction, and misery make for what reporters and their producers like to call "good television." So you continue to watch the gruesome footage and listen to the ongoing narrative, which essentially begs the question: How could the Israelis do such a thing?

Despite its military strength—or actually *because* of it—Israel is losing the PR war. Goliath isn't supposed to kill David, certainly not in this part of the world.

If Israel wasn't a full-fledged international pariah before today, thanks to the Qana video, it certainly is now. Weakness, after all, plays so much better on television than strength. Our sympathies naturally go to the poor victims—lifeless children, in this case—not the powerful military that just obliterated them. And this is precisely the problem with these pictures that I'm watching. They make for *such* "good television" that the viewer is distracted from the real story of this war.

Watching these poor men carry the bodies of dead children from the rubble makes it difficult to concentrate on the fact that it is Hezbollah—not Israel—that is the author of this tragedy. That it is Hezbollah that routinely violates the rules of war by hiding among civilians and using them as human shields. That it is the so-called Islamic "freedom fighters" who hide their weapons where children live. Watching these images, it is difficult not to forget that the Israelis, on the contrary, are the ones who try, as best they can in war, not to kill civilians.

As gripping as the pictures are, they lack a crucial element of good journalism: perspective. The camera embraces only what it *can* see. So we grieve for the children on our TV sets and their families, not for those two Israeli soldiers whom Hezbollah kidnapped, or the murder of their comrades—the singular event that touched off this war. These victims, the Israeli victims, are out of sight, and therefore also out of mind.

We are soon told by Israelis that a substantial number of rocket attacks on Israeli civilians during this war have come from rocket launchers in—surprise, surprise!—the very same village of Qana that is now the center of attention all around the world. The Israelis produce black-and-white spy footage showing trucks shuttling rockets around the streets of Qana. But these grainy Israeli images can't begin to compete with the crisp pictures of those dead children. So the focus this day, as most days, is on Israel's culpability.

Only the Israelis themselves—and the occasional conservative commentator—point out that there is reason to believe that Hezbollah might have hid weapons inside the apartment building the civilians were using as a shelter; that all this death and destruction perhaps was the result not simply of an Israeli rocket hitting the building but of the rocket blowing up Hezbollah's munitions and causing far more damage than would otherwise have occurred. Columnist Michelle Malkin made precisely that point to Bill O'Reilly. Yet even Bill, who understands the war on terror better than most who make a living in television, says it doesn't matter what the facts turn out to be—it won't make a bit of difference in the Arab world. Either way, the Arabs will manage to place the blame squarely on the shoulders of Israel.

Sadly, Bill is absolutely right. And herein lies another opportunity for journalists to ask some hard questions: What kind of world is it, in which facts mean nothing? Why are we meant to sympathize with Lebanon, and not Israel? And why is it that elites in and out of journalism tell us that Israel must be held to a higher standard? Is it because Israel is civilized and much of the Arab world isn't? Is it because even journalists, who are constantly on the lookout for racism, really believe Arabs are inferior to Jews? Is it because the elites expect nothing from the Arabs and when they get precisely that, they're not disappointed?

★

In the midst of all this, a friend sends me an e-mail, with his own questions. "Here's what I really want to know," he begins. "Why aren't the Lebanese people accountable for ridding their own culture of a scourge?

"It's either a) Hezbollah isn't considered a scourge, or b) Hezbollah isn't considered a scourge."

Good point, I'm thinking. Which is why we need stories—a drumbeat of stories, actually—asking a few more inconvenient questions: If Israelis need to think twice before firing at militants in civilian neighborhoods—which, by the way, they do—do Arabs need to think twice before hiding weapons among their own civilians—which, by the way, they don't? Should Hezbollah take any responsibility for the misery in Qana? Will Hezbollah and Hamas settle for anything less than the destruction of Israel?

But these are questions for some other day, if we're lucky. Today is a day for good television. For children being pulled from rubble. This is a day to be distracted from the real story and to concentrate on the pictures. This is not a day for perspective—or anything resembling critical thought, or even all the facts. This is not the time to point out that Israel withdrew from Lebanon six years earlier and got rockets and kidnapped soldiers in return, or that Israel pulled out of Gaza and got the very same thing. No, this is a day only for what the camera *can* see. Not for what it can't.

On Second Thought...

By now everybody knows politics has gotten way too nasty and way too partisan. Sure it was never patty-cake. But now, because news is everywhere—not just on TV and radio, but also on the Internet, on your cell phone, on your shoe, and on your underpants—you can't escape the muck no matter how hard you try.

But at least we don't have to take seriously the nonsense that flows from the mouths of our hyper-partisan politicians. We can say, "These slime merchants are destroying political discourse in the country and we refuse to pretend that they're the kind of people who should be taken seriously."

That's exactly what I said back in 2005, when I heard Senator Dick Durbin, the second-highest-ranking Democrat in the Senate, compare America's treatment of suspected terrorists at Guantanamo to the regimes of Hitler, Stalin, and Pol Pot.

Durbin, it seems, got his hands on an e-mail that an FBI agent had sent to his higher-ups, complaining about the way Al Qaeda suspects were being treated at the Guantanamo Bay prison camp. One victim, apparently, was being held in a very cold cell, barefoot, and was shaking when the FBI agent saw him; another was chained to the floor and forced to listen to loud rap music in a cell with the air conditioner turned off.

Granted, no one—not even a terrorist—should be forced to listen to rap music, no matter what the temperature or the decibel level. And no one is saying the other stuff was a walk in the park. But did any of it—even the "worst abuses"—really warrant the speech Durbin delivered on the floor of the United States Senate?

"If I read this to you and did not tell you that it was an FBI agent describing what Americans had done to prisoners in their control," Durbin told his fellow senators, and more important, the entire world, "you would most certainly believe this must have been done by Nazis, Soviets in their gulags, or some mad regime—Pol Pot or others—that had no concern for human beings. Sadly, that is not the case. This was the action of Americans in the treatment of their prisoners."

When I heard that, I figured here we go again. I thought it was nothing more than another pathetic, goofy, liberal Democrat simply doing what comes naturally: saying whatever it takes just to score a few cheap political points. After all, Pol Pot murdered nearly 2 million of his fellow Cambodians. Stalin threw his enemies into the gulag and it's estimated that between 3 and 6 million never made it out alive. Hitler killed 9 million in his concentration camps. Rap music is bad, but is it really *that* bad?

I may not have taken Dick Durbin seriously at the time, but I have just read several chilling news accounts about some newly uncovered atrocities at Guantanamo—atrocities committed by American military forces. And now I have second thoughts about Senator Durbin. Here's what I learned:

The prisoners at Guantanamo get three square meals a day. That's right: three nutritious meals seven days a week. As if that's not inhumane enough, during the Muslim holy month of Ramadan, the U.S. military staff at Guantanamo works "around the clock" to provide "Ramadan-specific" meals that include dates, nuts, and honey.

And we have the nerve to call ourselves civilized!

There's more. According to the *Los Angeles Times*, in order to quell protests about mishandling the Koran, American prison guards were ordered not to touch the holy book with their bare hands, but to wear medical gloves instead, out of respect. But now that's changed. Now, the *L.A. Times* reports, "only civilian Muslim interpreters are allowed to move and inspect the holy book during cell searches."

One American military official said, "There appeared to be no Islamic prohibition on non-Muslims handling the Koran." Still, "we want to make clear we show respect to Islam . . . that we do nothing that could be construed to be denigrating to the Koran."

If you're not ashamed to call yourself an American yet, you will be when you find out what other horrors are going on at Guantanamo—*in our name.*

It turns out that as a matter of official policy at Guantanamo, senior citizen terrorists—anyone over the age of fifty—is entitled to a colonoscopy exam performed by trained American doctors and paid for, entirely, by American taxpayers. *Oh, the shame of it all!* And President Bush has the gall to look the American people in the eye and say we're not torturing these poor people. Well, what, Mr. President, should we call it when some man wearing a mask sticks a tube up some Al Qaeda guy's ass? *A date?*

I began by saying I now have second thoughts about Senator Dick Durbin. And I do. Unfortunately for him they're exactly the same as my first thoughts. He *is* a pathetic, goofy, liberal Democrat all too willing to make exaggerated comparisons between rough treatment by Americans and a lot worse by the likes of Hitler and friends. That's not simply business-as-usual politics in pursuit of political points. It's hyper-partisanship that is hurting America.

So what can we do about it? Well, we might start by asking Dick Durbin. But that, I'm afraid, would be a waste of time. Forget about an answer. The real tragedy is that he and other hyper-partisans on the Left wouldn't even understand the question.

All the News
That Fits Their
Ideology
(Part 1)

My Head Wants to Explode

A friend of mine, a bright guy who follows the news closely, has just told me that he will no longer read the *New York Times*. It makes him angry, he says, and starts his day off all wrong. His exact words were: "Reading that paper makes my head want to explode." He used to read the *Times* religiously, but it's just gotten too ideological, he says—and not just on the editorial page.

He's got a point, of course. Journalists at the *Times* throw their liberal biases in all over the place—in movie reviews, in sports stories, even in articles about Norwegian seafood. I read a piece once in the *New York Times Magazine* that contained this gem: "If you see a whole monkfish at the market, you'll find its massive mouth scarier than a shark's. Apparently it sits on the bottom of the ocean, opens its Godzilla jaws and waits for poor unsuspecting fishies to swim right into it, not unlike the latest recipients of W's capital-gains cuts."

Does my friend really want to miss out on stuff like this? Where else will he find a story that combines tax cuts, monkfish, and Bush-only-cares-about-rich-people in one very short paragraph?

I, for one, love the biases in the *Times*. Okay, not the biases per se, but the way the journalists who work at the most important newspaper in the entire galaxy can find ways to jump through hoops and work their biases in. I love how shameless they can be about it; how they think we won't notice.

My all-time favorite example of ridiculous *New York Times* PC-ness *and* shameless hypocrisy all rolled into one is about those cartoons that ran in a Danish newspaper, which mocked the prophet Muhammad. One cartoon showed Muhammad wearing a turban in the shape of a ticking bomb. Another showed him at the gates of heaven telling suicide bombers, "Stop, stop, we have run out of virgins." This, of course, offended the sensibilities of many Muslims, who immediately tried to prove that theirs is a religion of peace by setting buildings on fire and vandalizing churches. And as the *Times* reported, "from Gaza to Auckland, imams have demanded execution or amputations for the cartoonists and their publishers."

This is what we infidels call "irony"—a concept, like tolerance, that means nothing to the homicidal maniacs who inhabit the world of radical Islam.

And even though the *Times*, like news organizations all over the world, gave plenty of coverage to the story, it never showed the actual cartoons that touched off the violence. On February 7, 2006, in an editorial, the *Times* explained why.

"The *New York Times* and much of the rest of the nation's news media have reported on the cartoons but refrained from showing them," the editorial said. "That seems a reasonable choice for news organizations that usually refrain from gratuitous assaults on religious symbols, especially since the cartoons are so easy to describe in words."

I say this not only as a journalist but also as someone who appreciates disingenuousness as much as the next guy: *Bull!* The cartoons should have been published, so readers would know exactly what touched off the widespread violence in the first place. You learn that in Journalism 101. Still, I understand the paper's dilemma—up to a point, anyway. No editor wants to needlessly offend people of faith—especially, as the *Times* says, when it's so easy to describe the cartoons in words.

So how do we explain a piece that ran in the very same *New York Times* just one day later? It was an article about the cartoons and "the power of imagery"—about how all kinds of art, through the ages, have provoked all sorts of emotions and reactions, including anger and violence. To illustrate the point, the *Times* ran a picture of a painting by Chris Ofili, called *Holy Virgin Mary*, a work of art that touched off a storm of protest when it went on display at the Brooklyn Museum in 1999. Why? Because the painting—a collage—shows the Virgin Mary surrounded by little cutouts from pornographic magazines and shellacked clumps of elephant dung.

So, let's see if I understand this: Showing the *Holy Virgin Mary* covered in elephant crap is okay, but showing cartoons that touch off worldwide mayhem would be disrespectful. I ask again: Does my friend who has stopped reading the *Times* really want to miss out on so much hypocrisy and other fun?

But let's pretend to take the *New York Times* seriously and ask a few questions: What about that editorial the *Times* ran *just twenty-four hours earlier*, about how the paper doesn't believe in "gratuitous assaults on religious symbols"? What about the high-minded stuff about how there's no need to show pictures when the images "are so easy to describe in words"? Why, when all is said and done, is it okay to show a piece of art that offends Christians but not a cartoon that offends Muslims?

The answer is simple. Radical Muslims are demented. When they get angry they either blow something up or cut somebody's head off. Christians, on the other hand, are fairly rational. When they protest they usually do it within reasonable parameters. So Muslims must be pandered to while Christians are fair game. No one will ever get into serious trouble for mocking Christianity or maligning its most sacred symbols.

So despite what the *Times* says, this isn't about respect. It's about fear. Fear that if the *Times* ran the cartoons, some of those radical

Muslims might actually blow up the *Times* building. In the end, the powers that be at the *New York Times*, who I'm sure fancy themselves courageous journalists, simply gave in to raw intimidation. The *Times* should have adhered to its own journalistic philosophy: give the reader as much information as possible. Run the cartoons *and* the picture of the Virgin Mary. In other words: Report the news!

And even if the mighty *New York Times* didn't have the courage to fess up to the obvious, one newspaper did, an alternative paper called the *Boston Phoenix*. Like virtually every other news outfit in America, the *Phoenix* decided not to publish the cartoons. But at least its editors were willing to tell the truth, explaining that they didn't run them . . .

> Out of fear of retaliation from the international brotherhood of radical and bloodthirsty Islamists who seek to impose their will on those who do not believe as they do. This is, frankly, our primary reason for not publishing any of the images in question. Simply stated, we are being terrorized, and as deeply as we believe in the principles of free speech and a free press, we could not in good conscience place the men and women who work at the *Phoenix* and its related companies in physical jeopardy.

Give the *Phoenix* credit for being honest, and for not hiding behind self-serving fairy tales about decency and journalistic responsibility.

An online column called "The Ethics Scoreboard" got it exactly right: "In the end, it may be that the most significant impact of the Danish cartoons was not the violence it unleashed or the cultural divide it exposed but how it revealed the pitiful lack of integrity, responsibility and courage among America's journalistic elite."

My friend, the one who stopped reading the *Times*, tells me that he agrees with every word. Still I recently asked him to reconsider. I tried to convince him that reading the paper really shouldn't make him angry. It should make him laugh. Shameless and clueless can be quite amusing, I assured him.

"No way," he replied. "If this were some paper in Podunk, I wouldn't give a damn. But the *New York Times* has tremendous influence. Powerful people who make important decisions read it and believe what they read. They give it respect. The *Times*, as much as I hate to say it, has enormous impact on our lives."

Unfortunately, he's got a point. Now it's *my* head that is about to explode.

And Then There's the News That's Unfit to Print...

I picked up the *New York Times* today and wasn't surprised by what I didn't see. Yesterday, I read a sad story on page one about how a search team had just found the bodies of two young American soldiers, one twenty-three, the other twenty-five, who had been "brutally tortured" and mutilated by insurgents who had captured them a few days earlier not far from Baghdad. Today, there was no follow-up on page one. Not a word. In fact, there wasn't a single story about the two men in the whole damn paper.

You can tell what a newspaper thinks is important by what it puts on the front page, and by how many times it puts it there. Take Abu Ghraib. The *New York Times* so far has run more than sixty page-one stories about how American soldiers abused Iraqi prisoners at that prison. And when the story broke in 2004, the *Times* ran thirty-two front-page Abu Ghraib stories—on thirty-two consecutive days! So, if you can tell what a newspaper thinks is important by what it puts on the front page, and by how many times it puts it there, to the editors of the *New York Times*, Abu Ghraib must be one of the most important stories of all time.

Let's not ignore the elephant in the room. Thirty-two page-one stories, day in and day out for more than a month, is not simply news coverage. It's a crusade. And no matter how honestly and objectively those stories were reported, together they amount to an editorial, masquerading as straight news.

With Abu Ghraib, the *Times* found new angles to report every day. The paper ran stories on the accusations . . . on the president's reaction . . . on how an officer suggested the abuse was encouraged . . . on command errors that aided the abuse . . . on how an Iraqi recounted the abuse by U.S. soldiers . . . on how the American guards at Abu Ghraib brought anguish to the unit's home in the United States . . . on an American soldier who was a "picture of pride" but became a "symbol of abuse" . . . on the connection between the abuses at Abu Ghraib and how "ill-prepared" and "overwhelmed" our soldiers are over there . . . on the trials of the accused American soldiers, which were about to begin . . . on the American head of the inquiry . . . on an Afghan's account of U.S. abuse . . . on prison policies that led to abuse . . . on a whistle-blower who "paints [a] scene of eager mayhem" . . . on another jail that served as an "incubator for abuses in Iraq" . . . on how the accused soldiers "try to shift blame in prison abuse" . . . on and on and on and on.

And those were just fifteen of the stories, just fifteen of more than sixty. It takes a lot of talent and enterprise to come up with so many stories covering so many different angles. So where, I wonder, was that same talent and enterprise, that same passion in trying to find *just a few* stories about the two young soldiers mutilated beyond recognition by the terrorists in Iraq? How did their buddies remember them? Did they leave sweethearts back home? I guess we'll never know, since the *Times* ran only one other article: a sidebar that appeared on the same day the paper reported the bodies had been recovered, about how both men were "Determined to Serve Country, and Willing to Face Danger," as the headline on page eight put it.

The *Times* is always telling us about the *magnificent* lives of people they find so *fascinating*, like those terribly important people who design handbags, and the ones who act in third-rate plays in dingy theaters way, way off Broadway. Don't two young American soldiers who died fighting for their country deserve the same respectful attention? But then these soldiers weren't sophisticated people. They didn't go to college. One even dropped out of high school. "Not our kind of people, or our readers' kind of people," you can practically hear the elitists saying at the *New York Times*.

But in reality we don't expect the *Times* to run sixty stories about these two brave soldiers the way it has run hundreds of stories about U.S. soldiers who embarrass their country. American valor never seems to interest the people who run America's "newspaper of record" even one-tenth as much as American dishonor does. In fact, from the *New York Times* we get precious few stories about anything good our soldiers do, and hardly any stories about American heroism.

I'd like to read more about those two young guys, and I sure as hell would like to read more about their killers. What makes some Muslims do such savage things in the name of their religion? Christians don't do these things. Jews don't, either. What is it about some of these Muslims that makes them different? Is it their holy book, their Koran? How did they become so dark, so absent of civilized values? I could handle thirty-two stories in thirty-two days, answering some of those questions!

But the editors of the *New York Times*, and many other liberals as well, are far more interested in Americans' misdeeds than in those of the terrorists. When the insurgents who killed those two young soldiers, for example, posted a video on the Internet, showing the mutilated corpses drenched in blood, the decapitated body of one of the soldiers with his head resting nearby and his chest cut wide open, the *Times* buried the story on page ten. Why didn't the paper put it on the front page, where it features every American "atrocity"?

Because focusing on America's faults fits the template, the preconceived storyline, the one that says, "Yes, the terrorists are bad, but so are we." Sure, even in liberal enclaves like the *New York Times* they acknowledge (in passing, anyway) that we're not *as* bad; we don't cut off anybody's heads, after all. We just throw them into places like Abu Ghraib and "torture" them. In the reprehensible words of Senator Edward Kennedy, "Shamefully, we now learn that Saddam's torture chambers reopened under new management—U.S. management."

This is what is known as "moral equivalence," which pretty much comes down to this: They do horrible things. We do horrible things. On its face, it is an intellectually lame argument, one that stems from nothing more than liberal hatred of George W. Bush. Does any serious person really believe that what went on in Abu Ghraib when Saddam Hussein was in power is the same as what goes on when the American military is in charge? Does any reasonable person really think that "Saddam's torture chambers reopened under new management—U.S. management"? Nothing speaks to the failures of modern-day liberalism—and its moral bankruptcy—more than this.

So keep those "We're the Big Bad Bully" stories coming, *New York Times*. And while you're at it, make sure you don't run too many pieces that make us weep for young, dead Americans whose bodies are dumped in the middle of the road, mutilated so badly that they can't even be recognized. Don't tell us too much about them; don't make them too human in your stories. Because if you do, we may actually start to understand that the real bad guys aren't in Washington but over there in the Middle East.

But I guess we're supposed to believe that the editors at the *New York Times* don't have a political agenda they allow to dictate their news coverage. Right! Once, the *Times* really did run "All the News That's Fit to Print." These days, "All the News That Fits Our Ideology" is more like it.

We Don't Need
No Stinking
Principles

It's a Wonderful Life. Or Not

Imagine how things would be different if President Bush had never taken us to war in Iraq.

Some four thousand American military men and women would still be alive.

Tens of thousands of Iraqi civilians would be alive, too.

Thousands and thousands more Americans and Iraqis would not be maimed.

Bombs would not go off—on the street, at police stations, in bakeries, and anyplace else you can imagine.

Sunnis and Shiites would not have savaged each other in what some called "sectarian violence" and others called a "civil war."

Billions spent on the war would still be in our national treasury, available for other things.

Children would still have their parents. Parents would still have their children.

What a wonderful life it would be for so many of us if President Bush never took us to war in Iraq.

There's more.

If we never went to war in Iraq, Saddam Hussein would still be alive and in power.

He would still be killing anyone who looked at him funny.

Kurds, if they said anything he didn't like, would be gassed again, their bodies left in the street where they had fallen, as a reminder to all the other "troublemakers" that the price of defiance is very high indeed.

Saddam loyalists would still be rounding up "dissidents" by the truckload—men, women, even young children—blindfolding them, putting bullets in their heads, and then dumping their bodies in unmarked mass graves.

"Enemies of the state" would still be tortured until they "confessed."

Saddam's "special agents" would still be raping Iraqi women to extract information from their "traitorous" husbands.

In other words, Saddam himself would still be a weapon of mass destruction.

And rest assured, Iraq would be rushing to build a nuclear bomb. Saddam could never sit back and let Iran have the only Muslim bomb in the Middle East.

Then the United States would have not one but two Muslim nations with nuclear weapons to contend with.

Yes, the world would be a different place if we never went to war in Iraq.

★

I wish President Bush had spent more time selling us on the humanitarian reasons for going to war, rather than stumbling onto them at the last minute. By the time he finally got around to talking seriously about human rights it sounded like an afterthought, something to take our minds off the fact that we couldn't find those other weapons of mass destruction.

By focusing on human rights sooner, he would have forced the hard Left to take a stand: Are you for the war or not? If not, he could have told them, be assured that all the crimes against humanity that you are always crying over will continue unabated. And they will go on, as uncomfortable as this may make you feel, if not exactly with your blessings then at least with your silent consent.

Perhaps they would have said that while human rights are important, while they oppose torture in all its nasty forms—at least in theory—this time around they are willing to look the other way, to remain silent, because the price to stop it is too high. That, pretty much, has been my position, uncharitable as it is. But, unlike my compassionate liberal friends I never pretended to be a humanitarian.

To this day I have not heard even one liberal—not anyone I know personally and not any national figure I've seen on TV—show so much as two seconds of unadulterated, *visceral* joy that thanks to the "incompetent" President Bush and his "misbegotten war" Saddam is no longer murdering, torturing, and raping his own people. Sure they acknowledge the obvious—that it's good that the tyrant is no longer around and in power—but they sound bored when they say it. I suspect it's because they hate George Bush more than they love their own ideals.

In his inaugural address on January 20, 1961, President Kennedy spoke eloquently of America's role in the world community. "Let every nation know whether it wishes us well or ill, that we shall pay any price, bear any burden, meet any hardship, support any friend, oppose any foe, in order to assure the survival and the success of liberty."

I cannot think of a single prominent Democrat today who would subscribe to a word of that.

I have a few questions, too, for my friends on the Right:

Some of you opposed this war from the outset. But many of you supported President Bush at every turn, more as an act of loyalty, I think, than one of conviction. Would you have supported the war in Iraq if Bill Clinton had started it?

Would you have supported the whole array of human rights and nation-building arguments President Bush has put forth in defense of the war if any Democrat—Clinton, Gore, Kerry, Edwards, Hillary, Obama . . . *any Democrat*—had made them? Would you have made so many excuses for so many blunders if a liberal had taken us into Iraq?

I'm afraid we know the answers to all those questions.

Which is why I feel like Alice in Wonderland, falling down a rabbit hole into a strange world where things keep getting curiouser and curiouser. Republicans support nation-building halfway around the world and Democrats oppose the only kind of war they like—a war to end crimes against humanity. Something is not right here.

If a liberal Democrat had taken us to war *not* just to find weapons of mass destruction, but also to create a democracy in a foreign country, and if that liberal Democrat had argued that all of this somehow would make Americans safer, Republicans would smack him silly. They would attack him relentlessly. They would accuse him of putting our young, brave American soldiers in harm's way. And for what, they would rightly ask? *So Iraqis can vote?* So the fanatics who would rather slaughter each other than come together to build a democracy would magically become our "allies in the war against terror"? *What conservative would buy that if a liberal Democrat got us into this mess?*

Yet most Republicans became embarrassing apologists for a disastrous war and couldn't find enough ways to defend the platitudes of our president—about how good will triumph over evil and how everyone deserves to live in a free country—even though it wasn't that long ago that President Bush and most Republicans thought nation-building was a policy embraced only by Democrats, liberals, and other unrealistic idealists.

Make no mistake: If Bill Clinton had dragged us into this war, the same conservatives who impeached him for lying about sex with an intern, would have impeached him all over again, this time for being a reckless commander in chief who went to war for all the wrong reasons.

★

Democrats say Iraq is the ghost of Vietnam. They may be right. When America left Vietnam, Democrats and other liberals were overjoyed. They had finally gotten what they had been demanding. Never mind that nearly a million South Vietnamese were murdered or died in "reeducation camps" or perished at sea on their way to freedom. The Left in this country, with a few notable exceptions, looked the other way, as if they had absolutely nothing to do with any of it.

I suspect liberals will be silent again if we leave Iraq on their timetable and "redeploy" our troops somewhere over the horizon. Who can say with any certainty what would happen then, but if the country turns into a giant killing field—far, far worse than when our troops were there—they will either pretend not to notice the blood-bath or blame it all on George W. Bush. But rest assured, they will act, once again, as if they had absolutely nothing to do with it.

And you wonder why so many Americans are fed up with politics.

A Rare
Politician
with Guts

Now that Tony Blair is done with politics in Great Britain, I wish he would come over here and run for president. I know. He can't. There's that part in the Constitution about how you have to be born in the United States to be president. Our loss!

The fact is, I love Tony Blair. He's a rare bird, a politician who isn't afraid to speak the truth, even when it's politically incorrect.

Take terrorism. The *Daily Telegraph* conducted a poll of British Muslims, asking about their attitudes toward terrorism; specifically their attitudes toward the London bus and train bombings, which left fifty-two people dead and hundreds more injured on July 7, 2005.

While a vast majority of the Muslims polled—88 percent—did not justify the bombings, 6 percent did. The percentage may seem small but it represents about a hundred thousand Muslims living in Britain. And who knows how many more felt the same way but weren't about to tell that to a pollster.

Twenty-four percent said even though they didn't actually condone the bombings, they did sympathize with the motives of the bombers. And 56 percent said they could at least understand why their fellow Muslims might want to set off bombs that kill innocent people.

The poll also asked Muslims if they agree or disagree with Tony

Blair's description of the bombers' ideas and ideology as "perverted and poisonous." While a majority—58 percent—agreed, a substantial minority—26 percent—didn't think so at all. And while most Muslims say they feel loyalty to Britain, nearly one in five British Muslims—18 percent—claimed to feel little or no loyalty to their country at all.

A year later, in 2006, the Pew Research Center took another poll of Muslim attitudes in Britain. This one showed that while 70 percent said they never supported suicide bombings, 24 percent said sometimes they did. Seventeen percent said they didn't think Arabs had anything to do with the 9/11 bombings in the United States.

You get the picture. So did Tony Blair.

A few weeks after the Pew poll came out, he met with key members of Parliament and told them that while government, obviously, had a role in stopping terrorism, law-abiding Muslims had an even bigger role.

"My view in the end is you cannot defeat this extremism through whatever a government does. You can only defeat it if there are people inside the [Muslim] community who are going to stand up . . . and not merely say 'You are wrong to kill people through terrorism, you are wrong to incite terrorism or extremism'—but actually, 'You are wrong about your view about the West, you are wrong about your sense of grievance.' . . . The whole sense of grievance and ideology is wrong—*profoundly* wrong. There may be disagreements that you have with America, with the U.K., with the Western world, but none of it justifies not merely the *methods*, but the *ideas* that are far too current in parts of the [Muslim] community. Now my view is that until you challenge that at its root, fundamentally, then you're always going to be left with a situation where people kind of say . . . 'Look we understand why you [terrorists] feel like this and you know we can sympathize with that, but you're wrong to do these things.' You're not going to defeat it like that. You're only going to defeat it if you say: 'You're actually wrong if you *feel* those things.'"

This is precisely why I'm such a fan of Tony Blair. He has guts to say out loud what the wimps and cowards on the Right and the Left are too afraid to say: that Muslims have it good in England. That they are not oppressed there or anyplace else in the West. That they need to stop viewing themselves as put-upon victims. That their "whole sense of grievance is . . . *profoundly* wrong."

Now, contrast that principled position with George Bush on another important issue, one with American political implications—immigration.

Our president sends his then chief political guru, Karl Rove, to the annual conference of a group called La Raza—in English, The Race—a Latino lobbying organization that supports all sorts of things that a supposed conservative like George Bush should be firmly against.

La Raza, for example, is funding a charter school in Los Angeles—a public school, mind you—whose principal, Marcos Aguilar, has said, "We [Mexican-Americans] don't want to drink from a White water fountain, we have our own wells and our natural reservoirs and our way of collecting rain in our aqueducts. We don't need a White water fountain. . . . And ultimately the White way, the American way, the neo-liberal, capitalist way of life will eventually lead to our own destruction."

Did I mention that George W. Bush's education department has shoveled $8 million to La Raza for charter schools like that one? Did I mention that in 2005 alone, La Raza inhaled more than $15 million in federal grants? So here's my question: What is Karl Rove doing pandering to these people?

Of course we all know the answer. He's out there trolling for votes for his fellow Republicans. Conservative principles? "*We don't need no stinking conservative principles,"* he might as well be saying.

And thanks to those alleged conservatives in the White House, our tax money is also going to the Dolores Huerta Preparatory High School in Pueblo, Colorado—a school named after the left-wing labor leader who in April 2006 told an assembly of high school kids in Tucson, Arizona, that "Republicans hate Latinos" and that "We didn't cross the borders, the borders crossed us."

As the columnist Michelle Malkin put it: "President Bush pays lip service to immigration enforcement and assimilation, while the White House sends Karl Rove to make nice with the separatist leaders of The Race and the Bush Education Department showers our tax dollars on radical . . . schools."

Maybe it's me, but I figure if you run as a conservative you ought to have the cojones to act like one. I understand that the immigration issue is complex. But certain parts of it are pretty simple. If you want to live in America, for example, assimilate. And instead of kissing up to separatist radicals and funneling millions of tax dollars their way, President Bush should be telling them—in plain English—that if they really think the American way, the capitalist way, is going to lead to their downfall, then "Go home. *Adios amigos!"*

Speak English, *Por Favor*

I just found out I'm living with a bigot. The villain is my teenage daughter, Catherine.

One day, the discussion in twelfth-grade American history class turned to immigration. My daughter suggested that anyone who wants to come to this country should learn how to speak English—and *pronto*. No one's forcing anyone to come here, she said, so if immigrants *choose* to live in America, the least they can do is learn our language.

For this, she tells me, she was nearly tarred and feathered by the other kids in class, many of whose parents are either from Cuba or someplace else south of the border. Not only should immigration be unlimited, the other kids said, but once they get here immigrants should speak whatever language they want. What's so special about English, they wanted to know.

You see, we live in a foreign country. Perhaps you've heard of it. It's called Miami, Florida.

This is the kind of place where a Jewish guy named Goldberg is called an "Anglo." Before I got here, the only time I heard that word was when it was attached to "Saxon" and "Protestant." In Miami, anyone who's not originally from Cuba or some other Latin American country is an "Anglo." We all look alike, you know.

In Miami, you can walk through entire sections of the city and never hear a word of English. Literally! When Cuban-Americans, many of whom have been in Miami for decades, get together in restaurants, or meet in department stores or supermarkets, odds are they're speaking to each other in Spanish. More and more, like my daughter, I feel like a foreigner in my own country.

Even in hospitals it's not easy to find people who speak English. An "Anglo" I know went in for lab tests and when she tried to ask the technician some very important questions all she got was "I no speak English too good." And don't try complaining. As a former colleague of mine, a Cuban-American cameraman at the CBS News bureau in Miami, used to say, "If you don't like it here, you can move." He wasn't kidding.

For what it's worth, there's a whole lot I like about Miami's immigrants. I like their work ethic. I like the fact that a lot of Cuban-Americans, for example, came here with just the clothes on their back and have done quite well in this country. I like that many of them go to church and hold on to traditional family values. If they can do all that, why can't they speak English in public?

The answer, of course, is that they can. They just won't. Critical mass has been established here in Miami. This is a Latin city. Miami has *mucho* Spanish-language radio and television stations and one very big Spanish-language newspaper. Adjust? That's what *minorities* do. *Minorities* are the ones who need to assimilate. And in Miami, the minorities are me and all those other "Anglos."

But Miami is only a piece of the American mosaic. The observation my daughter made about how immigrants should speak English if they want to live here might seem obvious in a small town in Iowa, but in a lot of other places, "Speak English" are fighting words. Like where? Well, think big chunks of California and Arizona and New Mexico and Texas and Colorado and even New York and New Jersey—to mention just a few.

Welcome to Multicultural America, where diversity—not language and not assimilation—is the highest priority. In Multicultural

America, English is no better than Spanish and assimilation means giving up your heritage. In Multicultural America, anyone who gets angry at the sight of half a million protesters in the streets of Los Angeles—many of them illegal immigrants waving Mexican flags and saying "We have a right to be here"—is a bigot.

And this is not simply the perceived wisdom in places with large Hispanic populations. You hear it anywhere with large *liberal* populations. Multiculturalism and diversity, after all, are part and parcel of the liberal worldview.

But here's the part that liberals, incredibly, don't seem to understand: Language does matter. English isn't optional, or at least it shouldn't be—not in the United States. Language is one of the things that holds us together as a nation.

A friend of mine, a successful businessman who came to America from Russia when he was twenty, with only a few dollars and a few words of English, tells me that he didn't start *feeling* like an American until he started *thinking* in English. "When you don't understand the language, you're on the outside. You're not part of the American culture. You feel like a transplant, not an American. How can you feel a part of something when you literally don't understand what's going on?" Assimilation matters, he says. Without it, "I might be *in* America, but I wouldn't be *an* American."

My friend understands the great immigration debate better than a lot of politicians do. He understands that if we allow too many immigrants in who don't care about assimilating, we're headed for trouble. We'll be stuck with a permanent underclass composed of perennial outsiders who will continue to put a strain on our welfare and health-care system and add to an already serious crime problem.

Conservatives, I think, get it—but that doesn't mean that all *Republicans* do. Too many of them are more concerned about their pals in business who depend on cheap immigrant labor—legal or otherwise. Just like Democrats, these gutless politicians are willing to pander, all in the good name of winning Hispanic voters.

So the president comes up with "guest worker programs" and "paths to citizenship." But, as my pal Burt Prelutsky, who lives in southern California, says, "Gussy it up any which way you like, it's still amnesty."

In his book *Conservatives Are from Mars, Liberals Are from San Francisco*, Burt writes: "Either the GOP is for more and more Mexicans coming across the border or it's not. But they should be warned that if it's the former, they run the very real risk of eliminating themselves as a major political party."

★

Conservatives aren't against immigration. They're against *illegal* immigration. And mostly, they're *for* assimilation. Stop the illegal flow first, a lot of us are saying. If that means building a fence, then build a fence. If it means putting troops on the border, then do that. Let the immigrants who are already here have a chance to settle in, to assimilate, *to become Americans and not just foreigners who are living here*. That can't happen if we continue to let Mexico export its poverty to the United States.

After we get control of our borders, then we can talk about "guest worker programs" and "paths to citizenship." But in the end, this should be the basic rule: If you want to live in the United States then embrace our culture. Speak English. Having tens of millions of people speaking Spanish in Mexico makes sense. In the United States, it's divisive. The political party that articulates this message best can win elections. I'm convinced it can even win over Hispanic voters who also believe in the rule of law and who don't just live here but have *become Americans*!

But this shouldn't be about what's good for Republicans or Democrats. It should be about what's good for America. If the millions and millions of immigrants coming north to the United States don't assimilate—because there are so many of them that they don't have to—our national identity will be torn apart. A society depends on shared values. And shared values include a shared language. The students in my daughter's American history class may not understand that yet. But they can be forgiven—they're only kids. What's the grown-ups' excuse?

★ ★ ★ ★ ★ ★ ★ ★ ★ ★ ★

If Katie Couric Is Jackie Robinson, Does That Make Bob Schieffer Martin Luther King Jr.?

No She Isn't

When Katie Couric took over as anchor of the CBS Evening News, Leslie Moonves, who runs the network, did his best to attach historical significance to the event. "She's the Jackie Robinson of network news," Maureen Dowd of the *New York Times* quotes him as saying.

Congratulations, Les! You just tied Don Imus (". . . it doesn't seem to me that a lot has changed since those marches in Selma") for first place in the dopiest statement in memory competition.

I get the comparison, lame as it is. Jackie Robinson broke the color barrier, Katie Couric the gender barrier. And what? They're both courageous Americans who made a difference? They both impacted the culture in an important and fundamental way? They both made millions of ordinary people reconsider what it means to be an American? Except they *both* didn't do any of those things. Only one did.

Most Americans of a certain age know the Jackie Robinson story, at least in broad strokes. They know he was forced to put up with humiliation that no human being should ever have to endure. When he ran out onto the ball field, he was verbally abused both from the grandstands and the other team's dugout. Players slid into second base, spikes high, trying to cut him. Pitchers threw at his head. On the field, he always had to wonder if someone was going to fire a rifle shot into his head. And this strong, proud man knew he couldn't fight back, because that would only make things worse. So he kept it bottled up. His hair turned gray. He was dead at fifty-three. But before he died, he changed America.

Now let's look at the *indignities* that Katie Couric must contend with. There's that pesky $15 million a year salary. And those nasty limousines that whisk her about town. And, when she's on the road, CBS actually makes her stay in the most luxurious suites at only the finest hotels. And don't forget those dreadful Park Avenue A-list dinner parties where fawning guests hang on her every word.

Forgive me, Les, you may know sitcoms and you may understand demographics, but you don't have a clue about Jackie Robinson.

When Jackie Robinson and his wife, Rachel, flew in from their home in California to spring training in Florida in 1946, a year before he joined the Brooklyn Dodgers, they stopped first in New Orleans. Hungry from the long flight, they asked where they could get some food. They couldn't, they were told. The airport coffee shop and restaurant served only white people. Then they were told they had been bumped from their flight to Pensacola to make room for a couple of soldiers. When they tried to get a room at the airport hotel, they couldn't. No blacks allowed.

When they finally got to Florida, they had to stay at the home of a black couple, because a local hotel wouldn't let them in. When he went to play ball, games were canceled, because local laws banned whites and blacks from competing on the same ball field. This was a man who had gone to UCLA and served his country in the United States Army. But as far as a lot of Americans were concerned, he was just another "nigger."

So, tell me again, Les, how exactly is Katie Couric like Jackie Robinson?

The problem is that Leslie Moonves inhabits a shallow subculture in America, a long plastic hallway where liberals run free and say the dumbest things. It's a place where they abuse history for no other reason than to satisfy their short-term needs.

This is a place where "Bush is a Nazi" passes for deep thinking. Instead of abusing history, they ought to try reading it. Then maybe they'd know a little more than "Hitler was a bad guy." Even before the war, anyone who was deemed an "enemy of the state" was fair game for the Nazis. Jews, socialists, trade unionists, the infirm, and anyone who disagreed with the regime—they all lived in terror. They were spit on when they walked down the street; they were beaten; their property was taken; their kids were made to inform on them; anyone suspected of harboring antigovernment thoughts was hauled off to concentration camps; the mentally retarded were killed by the thousands; and then, of course, there were the gas chambers.

How could anyone call George Bush a Nazi if they understood the evil of *any* of that?

I know, I know it's just what they say because they hate him. And all Leslie Moonves was doing was paying tribute to both blacks and women by comparing his new anchor to Jackie Robinson. But words count, and being promiscuous with them has consequences. Calling the president of the United States a Nazi—to satisfy short-term needs—disrespects the memory of anyone who saw the Nazis up close. And sorry, Les, but comparing a woman who gets paid big bucks to read the news to Jackie Robinson, a genuine American hero, disrespects everything Robinson stands for in America.

For once, I'll admit that Maureen Dowd got it right: Robinson represented a revolution; Katie Couric represents a promotion.

Who Got
Dan Rather?

Some people have delusions of grandeur.

Liberals have delusions of weakness.

And they love it. It animates them. It fuels their anger. It gives them energy to fight those dreaded conservatives, those right-wing bastards who run everything in our country into the ground and are so powerful and so evil that they even got rid of Dan Rather, a man whose only crime was reporting the news fairly and honestly.

Just one thing: It's not true.

June 20, 2006. The day Dan left the building. After forty-four years at CBS News, twenty-four of them as the anchor of its flagship broadcast, the *CBS Evening News*, Dan Rather was out, unceremoniously let go. That night I was on *Hannity & Colmes*, talking about it.

I had worked directly with Dan for many of my twenty-eight years at CBS News, and I had written about him in my book *Bias*. Alan Colmes, the liberal half of the team, asked the first question. "Conservatives kind of pushed him out. This was a political thing because they didn't like what happened with George W. Bush or this would not be happening, right Bernie?"

Well, no. But I understand why he asked. Liberals take it as an article of faith that Dan Rather was done in by those big, bad, powerful conservatives who had been gunning for him for years. Case in point: On the very same night I was on *Hannity & Colmes*, Craig

Crawford, a liberal political analyst, was telling Keith Olbermann on MSNBC that conservatives started a war with Dan Rather many years ago, and now "they won it with the demise of this man."

It was conventional wisdom in liberal circles that the end began for Dan when he went on the weekday edition of *60 Minutes* less than two months before the 2004 presidential election and reported that George W. Bush was a slacker back in his Air National Guard days in the 1970s. The story, as it turned out, was based on documents that CBS News could not authenticate and which conservatives generally believed were downright fraudulent. After that, Dan Rather was on borrowed time—time that ran out when CBS News finally caved in to right-wing pressure and sent poor Dan packing.

Wrong again.

Yes, it's true that conservatives had Dan in their crosshairs ever since he was a White House correspondent and went after Richard Nixon when the Watergate story broke. Nixon of course deserved it, but Rather's combative style didn't win him any friends on the Right. At a news conference in 1974, Dan got up to ask the president a question, and was greeted by a mixture of boos and cheers by the nonjournalists in the audience. When the buzz died down, Nixon asked Rather, "Are you running for something?" To which Dan famously replied, "No sir, Mr. President, are you?"

I never quite understood what that meant, but I knew it wasn't the kind of thing you say to a president of the United States, even one as smarmy as Nixon.

And yes it's true that conservatives were out there with pencil and paper to document every time Dan let his liberal biases slip into the news. But even Andy Rooney acknowledged that conservatives had a point. On Don Imus's radio show, Andy offered up his own postmortem on Dan's career: "My problem with Dan was always that you knew where he stood politically. . . . I thought he was a bad representative of the liberal side because he was so obvious with his opinions. There were just little words he used when he was on the air that made it apparent to everyone that he was a liberal Democrat."

And that came from one of his most liberal colleagues!

But the "fake document" story, which came to be known simply as Memogate (or, in some circles, Rathergate), took the charges of liberal bias to a whole new level. This time it wasn't "just little words" here and there. This time it was a story that could have affected a presidential election. This, as far as conservatives were concerned, was way over the line.

The story first broke on the Web, on conservative sites, but it didn't take long before it was everyplace. There was an in-house investigation, and soon after, Dan Rather lost his job as anchor of the *CBS Evening News*.

So, it's not entirely crazy to think that conservatives had done Dan Rather in. Except they didn't. Only one thing did Dan Rather in, the only thing that counts in television: ratings.

When Dan took over from Walter Cronkite in March 1981, the *CBS Evening News* was in first place, by a mile. But over the years the audience soured on Dan and he lost the lead. By the time his number came up, he had been firmly ensconced in third place, behind NBC and ABC, for more than a decade. For news executives, who worship in a church called Nielsen, this was sinful. Besides, over his twenty-four years in the anchor chair, Dan pulled in about $250 million in salary, give or take a few million. For a guy mired in the last place, this, too, was unacceptable.

So, long before conservatives ever uttered the word "Memogate," CBS wanted Rather out. Timing being everything, when the *60 Minutes* scandal hit, they seized on it as a golden opportunity to finally get rid of him.

But make no mistake: If Dan had been number one in the evening news ratings instead of the third man in a three-man race, he would still be at CBS News, still anchoring the evening broadcast— scandal or no scandal, liberal biases or no liberal biases. In television, power comes from ratings and Dan simply wasn't delivering.

But why wouldn't CBS News at least let him stay on at *60 Minutes*—as a kind of "thank you" for all his many years of service?

Sorry, conspiracy buffs, but politics had nothing to do with that decision, either. You see, Dan Rather committed an unforgivable sin in television: He got old. He was seventy-four when the scandal hit. *60 Minutes* has terrible demographics, or, in plain English, it has too many old viewers that advertisers don't give a damn about. CBS wanted young blood. Mike Wallace was already gone. Morley Safer was going. Dan Rather was high-priced excess baggage. So good-bye Dan, hello Anderson Cooper!

You might think that liberals would be relieved to hear that Dan's politics had absolutely nothing to do with his demise. No such luck! Liberals, we must always remember, love the underdog. They love the victim. Showing compassion makes them feel noble. Embracing weakness gives them strength. And so the liberal conspiracy crowd will forever believe that their boy, Dan Rather, got mugged, that he was a victim done in by those powerful, evil conservatives. Never mind that this is insane. Their perception is their reality!

★

The fact is, as I've mentioned before, liberals control just about every facet of our media culture except for talk radio. Liberals are the ones who make all the big decisions in network television news and at places like the *New York Times, Washington Post, Los Angeles Times, Boston Globe,* and a bunch of other bastions of so-called mainstream journalism. Think about it. If conservatives really had as much influence as liberals think, would CBS News have hired Katie Couric—a true-blue lefty whom conservatives distrust as much as, if not more, than Dan Rather? Would NBC News have hired Meredith Vieira, who not only marched in an antiwar demonstration but also said on her old television show that the war in Iraq was "built on lies"? Would ABC News have hired Charles Gibson, another anchor with liberal sensibilities?

Trust me. I know television news people. Of all the things management takes into account when choosing an anchor—looks, smarts, gravitas, likability, and a million other intangibles—they never factor in liberal bias. Never. They don't care about it. They don't understand it. They don't even think it exists.

In the history of network television news, I cannot think of one reporter or producer who was fired, suspended, reprimanded, or anything else, because of liberal bias. So rest easy, my liberal friends, you have nothing to fear except your paranoia. The only place conservatives hold power in Big Journalism is in the minds of anguished liberals.

And if they ever return to the real world, these liberals might actually see that it wasn't Dan's politics that got him in hot water. And that it wasn't conservatives who brought him down. With a little luck they may finally understand that it was Dan Rather who brought down Dan Rather.

What Courage?

The day those four CBS journalists got sacked in the wake of Memogate, I got to thinking about Dan Rather and one of his favorite words: *courage*.

Remember when Dan signed off his evening newscast with just that one word? Like so many other things that made a lot of us wonder if he was playing with all fifty-two cards—"What's the frequency, Kenneth?" . . . the on-air food fight with George Bush the elder . . . the time he stormed off the set in Miami and left the network with dead air for more than six minutes simply because women's tennis had run long and cut into his air time—this was one more thing that got people talking about him, and not in a good way.

For nearly twenty years, Dan's predecessor Walter Cronkite had ended the news each night with his signature, "And that's the way it is." Nothing controversial about that. Everyone gladly accepted it, especially since it was coming from "the most trusted man in America."

Dan was another story. "Courage" struck a lot of people—especially people who worked at CBS News—as, well, odd. The buzz wasn't good and so Dan dropped it after a while. But the word—and more important, what it represented—meant a lot to him. Dan Rather may have been making millions and living on Park Avenue, but he saw himself as a Texas cowboy, someone who stood tall for what he believed; someone who was loyal to his friends.

So what happened to *that* Dan Rather, I wondered, when four of his loyal colleagues, who worked with him on the George Bush Air National Guard story, either got fired or were forced to resign? How could a man of courage, a man who puts loyalty above almost everything else, have let them leave without going right out the door with them?

It seems to me that a loyal friend would have said, "Hey boss, if they go, I go." But Dan didn't say that. Apparently he needed to be part of CBS News more than he needed the respect of his colleagues. As Andy Rooney told Don Imus the morning after Dan lost his job, "I think most of us here think he should have quit. And I think he lost a lot of his friends around here when he failed to do that."

For forty-four years, CBS News and Dan Rather had been linked in a very deep and complex way. How many times over all those years had he said the words "Dan Rather, CBS News"? It was as if the name of the company was part of *his* name. It had certainly become a large part of his identity.

Being part of a worldwide news operation with a rich history, being on national television, and getting paid good money to do it, can be quite seductive. As Dan himself once said to me, "It sure beats working for a living." Some of us at CBS used to say that being on television was like being on crack. You got to really like it, and before you knew it, you were hooked. You think Dan was going to give it all up because four people he had worked with were being tossed overboard? Not a chance! Courage. What courage?

I understand that this may not sit well with conservatives who don't respect Dan Rather, and I understand that liberals simply may not believe me, but I truly liked the man during all those years I worked with him. He was funny and generous and would write you nice notes about your work, often signed, by the way, "Courage." And it is precisely because I liked him that I wish he had shown some dignity and resigned when his colleagues—the very people who worked to get *his* story on the air—got thrown out.

That would have been courageous. That would have been loyal. That would have been a noble act for which he would have been remembered for a long time. That's what a Texas cowboy would have done.

Instead he stayed, hoping against hope that CBS News would keep him on for years and years to come. And all he got for showing so little loyalty to his friends was a crummy year and a few months with CBS News. Followed, of course, by a shabby shove out the door.

★

In the end, Dan Rather did what liberals so often do. He talked a good game. But that's all he did—*talk*!

Liberals, at least a lot of the ones I know, think America is a dark place filled with all sorts of bigotry. So when they stand up for women's rights or gay rights or civil rights, they actually believe that they're beacons of enlightenment courageously standing up to the forces of evil—all those Republican red-state bigots who (they're convinced) want to turn back the clock a few hundred years. Inside their comfy liberal-elite bubble—at universities, in newsrooms, in publishing houses, at women's magazines, and at a whole bunch of other liberal enclaves—they endlessly reassure one another that they have more character, that they're *better* than those *right-wing yahoos* who are too stupid to think the way they do.

But when you get right down to it, they're just spouting words. They never have to put themselves on the line for any of their supposedly courageous stands. Just how tough do you really have to be to support liberal causes inside the liberal bubble where just about everyone you know holds the exact same position as you do? Standing in the middle of the newsroom at the *New York Times* and saying, "You know, I really like Bill O'Reilly and think he makes a lot of sense" would take courage. Standing up for late-term abortion or gay adoption or affirmative action in that same newsroom is nothing more than preaching to the choir—an activity that requires absolutely no courage.

What liberals don't seem to understand is that real courage requires real risk, sometimes even sacrifice. In my entire life I have never met even one liberal who said, "Give the job to the other guy instead of me—he's black." I have never met one liberal who said, "Let that minority kid into that Ivy League school instead of my kid—after all, my boy is upper-middle class, privileged, and white." It's easy to be liberal when you don't have to pay a price for your virtue.

Which brings us back to my old friend Dan Rather. This time he actually would have had to pay a price for his virtue. He would have had to quit his job to show solidarity with his colleagues who were forced out for putting his flimsy story on the air. *That* would have been courageous!

Dan, like so many other elites on the Left, talks a good game. They all stand for the "right" things. As long as it doesn't cost them anything.

In September 2007, Dan Rather sued CBS for $70 million. His old bosses, he claimed, made him a "scapegoat" for the phony document story and, in the process, damaged his reputation.

If he had shown some guts and quit when his colleagues got fired, his reputation might still be intact today.

Mike Wallace
in Mr. Rogers's
Neighborhood

There's an old line that used to make the
rounds at CBS News, about how the last thing the CEO of a major
corporation wanted to hear was "Mike Wallace on line one."

Anyone who has ever seen my former colleague in action gets
the joke immediately. Wallace was the Grand Inquisitor; the guy
you didn't want to face if you had something to hide. But I'm guessing that Ayatollah Khomeini didn't watch a lot of *60 Minutes* back
when he was leading the Iranian Revolution and holding American
hostages two and a half decades ago. I'm also guessing he didn't
know Mike Wallace from Kate Smith.

Big mistake. The ayatollah was no match for Mike when they sat
down in 1979. It was like Muhammad Ali going up against some
old, washed-up guy in the gym. Mike understood television. The
ayatollah was living in the seventh century; he didn't get any of it.
So Mike did what he does best. He calmly, gently, and, most of all,
politely hit Khomeini with a shot he never saw coming. "Imam,"
Mike said, "President Sadat of Egypt says what you are doing is,
quote, 'a disgrace to Islam.' And he calls you, Imam—forgive me,
his words, not mine—'a lunatic.' What have you to say to that?"

Who remembers the answer? And who cares? This was Mike
at his best, taking on a world leader and challenging his credentials—in this case, his very sanity.

But as they say: That was then and this is now.

On August 13, 2006, Mike went up against another Iranian leader, President Mahmoud Ahmadinejad. Mike asked some tough questions. But President Ahmadinejad was no patsy. He lives in the present. He's smart. He smiles a lot. And he's television-savvy. He understands the media at least as well as Mike does.

On at least two occasions Mike asked Ahmadinejad why he has said that "Israel must be wiped off the map." Please explain, Mike said. But Ahmadinejad never really did, except to finally say, as he has before, that Israel should be somewhere else, like Germany. Is this what he meant by "wiped off the map"—or was he just being *reasonable* for an American television audience?

Who knows? Mike also tried to ask him about Hezbollah missiles and rockets, which are furnished by Iran and, during the flare-up in the summer of 2006, were being lobbed into Israeli cities. But President Ahmadinejad didn't feel like answering that one, either. So he changed the subject.

Still, over the course of the interview, Mike got in more than a few good ones. But somehow it didn't matter. Somehow this man, who many fear is building nuclear weapons, possibly to drop on Israel, who has called the Holocaust "an overblown fairy tale," who presides over an autocratic regime, and who is seen as one of the greatest threats to world peace, came across as—no kidding—a fairly reasonable guy, at times even a likable one.

When Mike asked what his hobbies were, Ahmadinejad said studying, reading, and spending "quality time" with his family. *Quality time!* I almost fell out of my chair when I heard that one. You think you'd ever hear "quality time" coming out of Ayatollah Khomeini's mouth? No, this is the language of a modern man who understands the power of television and who knows how to speak American.

In fact, you got the impression that Ahmadinejad, unlike the ayatollah back in '79, was talking right past Mike and straight to the American people. He had a message to deliver, and he was going to deliver it no matter what Mike wanted to talk about. You got the impression, too, that Ahmadinejad knew more about America than Mike knew about Iran.

When the Iranian president told us what a shame it was that 1 percent of the American people are in prison, Mike just let it go. He didn't counterpunch. It would have been nice if he had said, "Yes, Mr. President—and please forgive me—but how many Iranians has your regime locked up in your own prisons, simply because they don't agree with you or the mullahs who run your country?" It would have been nice, too, if Mike had asked, "Why does your regime, Mr. President, still stone women for the crime of adultery?" But Mike didn't ask about any of it. Give that round to Ahmadinejad.

The Iranian president also fretted about how unfortunate it was that 45 million Americans don't have health-care insurance. "That," he said, "is very sad to hear." For a second or two I thought I was listening to Phil Donahue or Hillary Clinton. I mean, you just *know* that every liberal tuned in to *60 Minutes* was nodding in agreement. "He's not such a bad guy, after all," they were probably thinking. "So much more reasonable—and *intelligent*—than Bush."

In fact, instead of seeming like a modern Hitler (a not unreasonable comparison, given that one wanted to exterminate all the Jews while the other wants to wipe Israel off the map), President Ahmadinejad came across as, well, a fairly typical, run-of-the-mill liberal showing compassion for criminals and people without medical insurance. That's not a shot at liberals. Really. Just an observation that Ahmadinejad shares a lot of their views, mostly about what a mess President Bush has made of things, both foreign and domestic.

I listened carefully as the Iranian president laid out his position on the war in Lebanon and on the Bush policy in Iraq, and I could not detect any significant difference between his views and those held by a lot of blue-state liberals, especially the liberal intellectuals on our college campuses. "Killing innocents is reprehensible," he told Mike Wallace. "Why are Americans killing Iraqis?" he asked. Hey, I just heard the same thing on Air America.

To his credit, Mike didn't let up—though I thought there was way too much laughing and smiling going on between the two. At one point, Ahmadinejad was handed a note by one of his people and Mike wanted to know what it said. Turns out, the Iranian president's handler wanted to make sure his boss's jacket was neat. This prompted Mike to ask, "Are you a vain man?" "Sometimes you have to look your best," Ahmadinejad replied. "That is why I comb my hair." There was smiling, laughing, and finally Mike saying: "Let me assure you, you look your best." What, no hug, Mike?

Score that round for Ahmadinejad, too.

In the end, all a reporter can do is ask the tough question and let the subject answer. If he doesn't, you can try again. But at some point, you have to move on. And that is precisely what Mike and *60 Minutes* should have done—but didn't. They should have moved on and found some people who know the real Mahmoud Ahmadinejad—not the made-for-television Mr. Rogers version. They should have found some people to fill in the blanks; people who could paint an alternative picture of this man. They should have rounded up a few Iranians living in exile—the ones who must have been throwing shoes at their television sets during the interview—and asked them what really makes him tick.

But there were no exiles in the piece. No Israelis, either. No one from Amnesty International to talk about how repressive the Iranian regime really is. Nor were there any historians, people who would have been able to say that Ahmadinejad is not the first leader of an undemocratic country to speak in platitudes about how much he longs for peace, justice, and fairness. Read *Berlin Diary* by William L. Shirer, who along with Ed Murrow covered World War II for CBS News, and you'll learn that Hitler spoke the same way.

Score another round for the Iranian president; enough for him to win the night on points.

Twenty-seven years ago it didn't matter what Ayatollah Khomeini told Mike Wallace. We only remember Mike's question about whether or not the ayatollah was a lunatic. Now, the tables are turned and it is the questions that don't matter—especially when the subject smiles and makes an end run around them, replying with such soft and fuzzy answers as, we need to "love all people."

None of this is about liberal bias.

Not the way we usually use the term, anyway. It is, however, about liberal *sensibilities*—the mind-set that dominates the thinking at mainstream news organizations.

Consider this: A *60 Minutes* profile of Bill O'Reilly—also done by Mike Wallace—included clips of Bill jousting with liberals like Michael Moore, *New York Times* columnist Paul Krugman, and Al Franken—giving some of O'Reilly's biggest enemies an opportunity to get in their licks. Wallace's piece about the Fox News channel and its boss Rupert Murdoch included a section with his liberal competitor, CNN founder Ted Turner, who told Mike that Murdoch "looks down his nose at good, honest journalism."

But we get no other voices in the profile of Ahmadinejad? He gets treated as if he were Winston Churchill—or Nancy Pelosi. If his name were Limbaugh instead of Ahmadinejad, you can bet he'd get more scrutiny from *60 Minutes*. Instead, CBS News allowed, and even enabled, Ahmadinejad to present himself as a reasonable, even compassionate, man in tune with liberal values on health care and prison reform. Mike let him smile and laugh and define himself as someone who *cares*—just what you have to do in our media culture to come off as likable and pick up new allies in the process— the same allies he is hoping will pressure George Bush to get out of Iraq, stop supporting Israel, and lighten up on Iran so they can continue building their nuclear "power plant."

★

Nevertheless, even at eighty-eight, Mike is still one of the best out there. But I'm afraid my old colleague, the Grand Inquisitor, got played. For, over the years, dangerous men like Ahmadinejad have learned how to use the media for their own good. They have gotten quite sophisticated.

Unfortunately, "Mike Wallace on line one" doesn't scare anybody in Tehran.

Uncomfortable Questions

Jesse Jackson wants a full-scale investi- gation of what went wrong after Hurricane Katrina hit New Orleans and other parts of the Gulf Coast. We established a "study group" to find out what went wrong in Iraq, he says, and we should do the same with Katrina.

Just what we need: another commission to study another problem.

Most of us already know that the government screwed up during Katrina. But screwing up is what governments do. So, should we really be shocked when FEMA shows up late? Or when the mayor of New Orleans doesn't have a plan to use hundreds of city school buses to get people out of town ahead of the storm?

Maybe some naive liberals expect competence from government, but conservatives—and anyone else who has gotten old while waiting in line at the post office or has driven his car into a pothole as big as Cleveland—know enough to expect very little from our wonderful public servants. In other words, anyone who thinks government is the answer to any important question obviously has had little experience with government.

So when President Bush arrives to tour the devastation, puts his arm around FEMA director Michael Brown, and says, "Brownie, you're doing a heck of a job," you have to wonder what in the world he's thinking. All that was missing was the MISSION ACCOMPLISHED banner.

But, as we soon learned, that pat on the back was more like a kiss on the cheek—by a Mafia don. Ten days later, Brownie got canned and went into business for himself—*as a consultant on disaster planning*. Karl Marx was right: First we get tragedy, then we get farce.

But replacing Michael Brown, necessary as it was, was only a first step, and a very small one at that. Government, regardless of which bureaucrat is running which agency, can do only so much. We can blame FEMA all we want, but in the long run it doesn't get us very far. Neither does pinning the misery in New Orleans on indifference brought on by racism. But that, of course, hasn't stopped the pundits from invoking racism every chance they get.

The real problem, I'm afraid, is much more complex. The real problem is the *culture* of the underclass—a culture of failure brought on by self-destructive behavior that turns its citizens into helpless victims who can't cope with a whole array of problems, Katrina being just one of them.

How do you fix that?

★

A while back, in the middle of the Katrina mess, I caught anchorman Aaron Brown, then with CNN, mixing it up with conservative media critic Brent Bozell, who had just written a column that said: "A truly deplorable aftermath of Katrina is the far left's attempts to stir up racial divisions and the news media's fanning of those flames. Both should be roundly condemned."

But there were "perceptions" of racism, Aaron Brown pointed out. Didn't that make it a legitimate subject of media inquiry?

"Perception is dangerous if it's not rooted in reality," Bozell said. And "by dangerous I mean an accusation that splits the seam of the cultural fabric of the country." The media have a responsibility "to go to those people [making the accusations of racism] and say, 'put up or shut up.'"

But why, Brown wanted to know, did Brent Bozell think that he—the anchorman—was a "race baiter" simply because a few days earlier he had asked a black congresswoman if she thought "black America is sitting there thinking: 'If these were middle-class white people, there'd be cruise ships in New Orleans, not the Superdome?'"

"I think it is the role of the reporter to ask the question, even when the question is uncomfortable," Aaron Brown said.

I couldn't agree more. That is precisely the role of the journalist—to ask uncomfortable questions. Too bad it doesn't actually work that way. Not when the subject is race. That's when we put a Mardi Gras mask over the problem and make believe it isn't there.

There is no subject that journalists fear more than race in America. None.

Back when I was a CBS News correspondent, a colleague reported a story for the evening news, about the reemergence of the chain gang in Alabama. He showed a typical chain gang, composed of twenty prisoners. Nineteen were black. This touched off a major sensitivity crisis in New York. The field producer was warned "to be more careful next time." Never mind that the chain gang was in Alabama, not Sweden. When it comes to race, political correctness trumps factual correctness every time.

The problem is that reporters tend to be liberal and liberals don't really want to ask "uncomfortable" questions about race, because the entire subject of race makes *them* uncomfortable. Unless, of course, it's framed in the usual safe, familiar terms: Black people as victims of white racism. This way, reporters can be on the side of the angels. They can win the approval of black folks, which, more than anything else, makes them feel virtuous about themselves. White liberals in general, and journalists in particular, think they need permission from the black establishment before they're allowed to ask the truly uncomfortable questions. Rest assured, it will be a long, long wait.

Yes, it's a painful truth that many of the problems plaguing poor black Americans today can be traced back to slavery and segregation, back to years and years of oppression that tragically have created a crucible for destructive behavior. But the fact is that neither the slaveholders nor the segregationists are coming back to fix anything. And, when it comes to fundamental change, we can't count on the government, either. No, these are obstacles that must be overcome primarily *by the disadvantaged themselves*—a very difficult task so long as liberal enablers point fingers at everyone else and conservatives are too frightened to even broach the subject.

Despite the clichés, the reason so many black people were left in such dire straits in New Orleans wasn't because they're black. They were stranded because they're poor. In places like New Orleans, that may seem to be a distinction without much of a difference— but it's a very important distinction nonetheless. Some good might actually come from the tragedy of Katrina if journalists (and politicians) start asking some tough, uncomfortable questions about why those people remain so poor at this time in our history—even after millions upon millions of other black Americans moved out of poverty and into the middle class.

We need more stories about how poverty—while historically the result of unemployment, low-paying jobs, and yes, the loss of opportunity because of racism—today is something quite different. As David Ellwood of Harvard has put it: "The vast majority of children who are raised entirely in a two-parent home will never be poor during childhood. By contrast, the vast majority of children who spend time in a single-parent home will experience poverty."

William Galston, a domestic advisor to President Clinton, made the same point. To avoid poverty, he said, you have to do three things: finish high school, marry before having children, and marry after the age of twenty. Only 8 percent of people who do this, he says, wind up poor, while 79 percent who *fail* to do it end up in poverty.

For too long, questions about behavior—*dysfunctional* behavior—have been out of bounds. They're seen as racist; as blaming the victim. But if reporters don't ask uncomfortable questions, how are we going to understand why things go wrong?

So, here are a few suggestions for my fellow journalists, which will come in handy not just when another hurricane hits and leaves poor black people stranded all over again, but also whenever they do any important story concerning race in America:

★ Why is the black illegitimacy rate so high in this country today—somewhere around 70 percent—when it was much lower (10 to 20 percent) in the 1950s, a time when institutional prejudice was far more widespread than it is today?

★ How is it that black Americans of those earlier generations—people who had to deal with blatant racism every day—were able to do the right things and keep their families together, while many of those who came of age after the 1960s have succumbed to one pathology after another?

★ What chance in life do babies have when they're born to fifteen-year-old girls?

★ Why do about half of all black inner-city kids drop out of high school?

★ Does a kid who drops out, and can't speak proper English, stand much of a chance of getting a good job and escaping a life of poverty?

In other words, did the desperate victims of Katrina, mostly young, black people, lead the kind of dysfunctional lives that inevitably lead to poverty? Is that why they were left stranded—at the mercy of incompetent government? On too many occasions I heard young women telling TV reporters that they had to find milk or water or diapers for their babies. Not once did I see a husband in the shot.

So, in the wake of Katrina, while Jesse Jackson and his cronies are focusing on what the government did wrong, shouldn't we also ask a few uncomfortable questions about what the victims of the hurricane have been doing wrong for years, which left them so vulnerable? After all, it wasn't just rich white folks who made it out of town before Katrina hit. Middle-class blacks escaped, too.

I understand that to ask these questions while people are fighting for their lives would be callous and insensitive. That wasn't the time. But at some point, journalists *must* start a serious national conversation on race in our country. Without hard questions it's too easy to fall back on the old feel-good liberal platitudes about how "racism" is the root of all our troubles and about how more "diversity" is the solution. The only way to put an end to this cycle of dishonesty and denial is to begin asking uncomfortable questions and speaking uncomfortable truths. And if the race mongers want to yell "racism"—then let them yell all they want. Wimpy politicians won't stand up to these people. They're too afraid. Journalists have to.

★

To his credit, Tom Brokaw broke the mold, in a special about race, one year after Katrina. The program was called "Separate and Unequal"—just the kind of title you'd expect liberal media types to come up with—but Brokaw went beyond the usual liberal clichés and spoke to dozens of people who helped explain why blacks in places like Jackson, Mississippi, have remained separate and unequal forty years after the civil rights movement.

Brokaw went to a newspaper in Jackson—"once the racist voice of the white establishment"—and interviewed its editor, a black man whose father was a sharecropper. Ronnie Agnew was the man's name, and he told Brokaw: "I'm a strong proponent of the lack of excuses because I guess I'm a product of the lack of excuses."

Brokaw asked a black woman, "When it comes to the African-American family, what would you change?" And she told him something you don't often hear on national television: "I think the one thing that we need to work on is accountability. They just allow people to get off too easily. That's why we have grandparents who are raising, you know, grandchildren. We have sisters who are raising sisters. Because our parents, they're not stepping up to the plate."

Brokaw also spoke to an honor student at all-black Lanier High School in Jackson, who told him that the problems she faced in school came not from old-fashioned racism but from black kids who gave her a hard time because she took her schoolwork seriously—and told her she wasn't "ghetto enough."

Good for Tom and good for NBC for putting this kind of stuff on the air. We need to hear more of it, and not just from people like Bill Cosby or Juan Williams, who has written a book about the absence of black leadership and the culture of failure; or from black conservatives who have been preaching the gospel of personal responsibility for a long time now. We need to hear a whole chorus of voices of ordinary black Americans like those folks in Jackson, Mississippi. We need to hear the voices of white liberals on the virtue of hard work and the pathology of self-destruction. We need to hear from conservatives, too, who have remained far too silent.

Yes, the government has certain important obligations to its citizens. And yes, the government failed and has to make sure it learns from its mistakes. But so do the *people*, the actual victims of disasters like Katrina. And without more journalists asking uncomfortable questions, it's not likely to happen.

★

In the end what we have here is indeed racism—*white liberal racism*. Why? Because this failure to ask the truly uncomfortable questions shows just how much less concern liberals have for black kids than white kids. If the kids whose lives were being destroyed in New Orleans and a hundred other American cities were white, I'm pretty sure we'd be getting a lot more than platitudes and finger-pointing. We'd be asking the hard questions and demanding real answers. Why are these kids being raised in drug-infested neighborhoods by single parents? Where the hell are the fathers? Why are thirteen-year-old girls having babies? Why is it a badge of honor for a young man to go to prison? *Why are these kids and their parents so damn dysfunctional?* Liberals would never tolerate any of this in the white America they live in. But it's easy to be "virtuous" when it's someone else's kids whose lives are being destroyed.

Why do they never ask these questions? That's the question that should make white liberals more uncomfortable than any other.

All the News
That Fits Their
Ideology
(Part 2)

It's in Their DNA

Imagine, if you possibly can, that Arthur Sulzberger, the publisher of the vaunted *New York Times*, is delivering a commencement speech, and telling this to the graduating class of 2006:

> Make no mistake, you are graduating into an America at war. We are at war with Muslim fanatics who want to kill every one of us. They are a dark force in the world—the darkest force, in my opinion, since the Nazis. And we must respond to them the way your grandfathers and grandmothers responded to fascist tyranny so many years ago. We must unite! And we must destroy them!

Of course, you'd have to be smoking something illegal to think the publisher of the *New York Times* would actually say anything like that.

In fact, *this* is what Arthur Sulzberger *actually* told the graduating class at the State University of New York at New Paltz on May 21, 2006:

"I'll start with an apology," he said, explaining that his generation "had seen the horrors and futility of war and smelled the stench of corruption in government," referring to Vietnam and Watergate. "Our children, we vowed, would never know that. So, well, sorry. It wasn't supposed to be this way. You weren't supposed to be graduating into an America fighting a misbegotten war in a foreign land."

What the publisher of the *New York Times* (and other liberals) calls a "misbegotten war" President Bush (and many conservatives) calls a battleground in the global war on terror. And just thirty-three days after the commencement speech in Upstate New York, Bill Keller, the executive editor of the *New York Times*—who reports to Arthur Sulzberger—ran a front-page story on one facet of that larger war, a story about a secret government program that tracks money as it moves from one terrorist to another. He did this even after prominent Republicans *and* Democrats asked him not to, because, they said, it would hurt our country in the war on terror.

Of all the reasons Bill Keller gave for running that story—questions about the legality of the program, lack of congressional oversight, and the always-popular people's right to know—he left out the most important one of all: It was a good career move.

You think the *government* has secrets? Here's a secret the liberal media don't want you to know: If it's a close call between protecting the national security by *not* publishing government secrets . . . or publishing them because you know you'll get brownnosing points from your boss (not to mention fawning accolades that you crave from your friends in the media), publishing the secrets beats *not* publishing the secrets almost every time.

I'm not suggesting, even for a moment, that any of this is conscious. It's just that in the universe of big media, careerism is always there, right beneath the surface. It's part of their DNA.

But, you may be saying, aren't those news executives who work at major media news organizations ideologues? Yes, some are. But ideology comes in second. Career comes in first.

You might also ask, but doesn't the *Times* run those secrets on page one because it doesn't trust George Bush and has precious little respect for his presidency? Of course, the *Times* mistrusts George

Bush. But that's still reason number two. Again, career comes first.

Bill Keller is absolutely correct when he says there is a large wall that separates his domain at the *Times*—the supposedly objective news side of the paper—from his boss's domain—the opinion side. But the real world is more complicated.

At CBS News, I once suggested we do a story about conservative allegations of liberal bias in the news. I told my boss I wanted to interview Dan Rather, then the anchor of the evening news. The president of CBS News reluctantly green-lighted the story—on one condition: that I agree *not* to ask Dan "any tough questions." The news president, who wasn't nearly as powerful as the anchorman, wasn't about to put himself in a bind by letting me do a story that might offend Dan. It's the mantra of big-time journalism: Career always comes first. (Just so you know, with that insane restriction, I refused to do the story.)

Which brings us back to that commencement speech in May 2006. If Arthur Sulzberger had told those seniors, "We must unite against the terrorists who want to kill us and we must destroy them," do you think Bill Keller, thirty-three days later, would have run that terrorist-money story on page one?

Neither do I.

And one more little secret that they don't want you to know about at the *Times*: They're in the Pulitzer business over there on West Forty-third Street, just as the Hollywood crowd is in the Oscar business. And there's no better way to win a Pulitzer than by running stories about secret government programs that supposedly are eroding our civil liberties in the name of the "so-called" war on terror. You think Bill Keller thinks about that when he runs his front-page secret stories?

So do I. It's a good career move.

Clueless in Manhattan

"When I sell liquor, it's called bootlegging," Al Capone once said. "When my patrons serve it on silver trays on Lake Shore Drive, it's called hospitality."

It's also called hypocrisy, which, of course, was exactly the point the Chicago gangster was trying to make. And while the elites haven't quite cornered the market on hypocrisy, they have always been especially good at it. Which brings us—where else?—to the *New York Times*.

The elites at places like the *Times* are different from ordinary Americans, which, trust me, is very good news for ordinary Americans. *Times* people see themselves as smarter, more sophisticated, and generally *better* than everyone else; and this superiority complex allows them to be as arbitrary and inconsistent as they need to be and not worry about losing their moral standing along the way. So they can rail against vouchers that would let poor black kids go to private schools while they send their own children to expensive preppy academies. They can sing the praises of affirmative action then do whatever it takes—from getting high-powered friends to pull a few strings with the college admissions committee to coughing up a bundle of cash for the school's endowment fund—to make sure their little sweetheart isn't hurt by the very same affirmative action they publicly claim to love so much. Or they can righteously bemoan the state of affairs when conservatives launch a campaign against an anti-Reagan movie but willfully ignore a similar campaign when liberals are the ones making threats.

What do I mean?

In 2003, the editorial writers at the *Times* detected a "Soviet-style chill" in the air, a chill that posed a grave threat to America and everything it stands for. The villains were—who else?—conservatives!

What caught the attention of the *Times* was the controversy surrounding a CBS docudrama about Ronald Reagan, a movie that had conservatives up in arms. The screenwriters had put words in Reagan's mouth he never actually said, words that made him look dumb and mean-spirited. Coming as it did when the former president was suffering from Alzheimer's and couldn't defend himself, the *Times* was sympathetic—uncharacteristically so—to the concerns of Reagan's many admirers. "It is not difficult," the editorial said, "to see why people close to Mr. Reagan would be upset that the script quoted him, for example, on the subject of AIDS sufferers as saying, in an invented quotation, 'They that live in sin shall die in sin.'"

But there's just so much sympathy the *Times* can muster for conservatives. So the editorial went on to say, "It should have come as no surprise that conservatives, protective of Mr. Reagan's image at all times, would launch one of the fierce assaults that have become so familiar whenever the right wants to scare the media on an ideological question."

Yes, we all know how totalitarian those closed-minded conservatives can be—actually demanding that the network portray Mr. Reagan *accurately*. What nerve!

In the end, CBS gave in to the pressure and yanked the movie, shuffling it over to Showtime, the cable channel owned by the same parent company as CBS, where far fewer people would see it. An all-out war with the Right was diverted.

But peace, such as it was, came at too high a price as far as the editorial board at the *New York Times* was concerned. Ronald Reagan's "supporters credit him with forcing down the Iron Curtain," the editorial continued, "so it is odd that some of them have helped create the Soviet-style chill embedded in the idea that we, as a nation, will not allow critical portrayals of one of our own recent leaders."

Ah, there it is! The ever-present liberal fear that not only do conservatives have absolutely no respect for the other guy's opinion but the delusion that they can't wait to impose their totalitarian "Soviet-style" worldview on open-minded people everywhere. It's good to see that the *New York Times* is troubled by Soviet-style chills now that the Soviet Union has crumbled and it's safe to say such things, especially about conservatives in America. We admire the courage over there on West Forty-third Street, belated and meaningless as it may be.

Now cut to 2006 and another controversy over another television docudrama, this one on ABC, about the events leading up to 9/11. This time the screenwriters didn't distort history to make a conservative Republican look bad. This time they manipulated the facts to make Bill Clinton look bad.

Once again the *Times* editorialized on the pitfalls of docudramas. "Perhaps the entertainment industry will come up with a few lasting lessons from the outcry over ABC's 'dramatization' of the events leading up to the terrorist attacks on 9/11," the editorial began. "One suggestion: when attempting to recreate real events on screen, you do not show real people doing things they never did."

I'm with the *Times* on this one. I don't like it when screenwriters try to improve on history just for ratings. Personally, I rarely watch docudramas. And when I do, I'm always wondering where the docu ends and the drama begins. They leave the journalist in me feeling uneasy. What a coincidence! So does the *New York Times*.

You'd think that by now I'd be used to the paper's abandonment of principle in favor of naked partisanship. But the *Times* always manages to catch me off guard. In 2003, remember, the *Times* warned us about those "fierce assaults" by Reagan supporters who were out "to scare the media." So it's not crazy to expect a little outrage from the same *New York Times* when liberals in 2006 do the exact same thing; when they launch their own "fierce assaults" and mount their own campaign "to scare the media." Right?

Well, no.

Let's start with five liberal Democratic U.S. senators—including Harry Reid, the Democratic leader in the Senate—who fired off a rocket to the head of the Disney Corporation, which owns ABC, demanding that the docudrama be canceled outright. "We urge you, after full consideration of the facts, to uphold your responsibilities as a respected member of American society and as a beneficiary of the free use of the public airwaves to cancel this factually inaccurate and deeply misguided program," the letter said.

Talk about your strong-arm tactics. Tony Soprano would have been embarrassed. When five U.S. senators tell a broadcaster that he's the "beneficiary of the free use of public airwaves," that's not a friendly reminder. It's a barely veiled threat. Yet we got nothing in the *Times* editorial about this letter. No indication that the letter even exists. So, of course, we get no fretting about the "Soviet-style chill" that troubled the *Times* so much back in 2003.

And then there was Bill Clinton, who also hated the docudrama. Two of his closest associates—his lawyer and the head of his foundation—wrote a scathing letter to ABC, demanding that the network fix "the egregious factual errors" in the movie or "pull the drama entirely."

Too bad the *Times* was still suffering from amnesia and "forgot" to make any mention whatsoever of this letter, either—even though it was written on behalf of the former president, whose wife, you may recall, is an important U.S. senator who may be the next president of the United States, with all the clout to punish enemies that goes with the job. All of this escaped those fair-minded people who write editorials at the *Times*. Once again they forgot to wring their hands the way they did when conservatives were doing the so-called bullying. Once again they forgot to worry about that scary "Soviet-style chill." This time, all we got from the *Times* was silence.

Let's be fair, though, and acknowledge that there has been plenty of hypocrisy to go around. Conservatives who complained when fictional dialogue made Reagan look bad had no problem when fictional dialogue made Clinton look bad. And liberals who were outraged over the distortions in *The Path to 9/11* docudrama were quite comfortable with the distortions in the Ronald Reagan movie.

But they're partisans who don't pretend to stand on principle. The editorial writers at the *Times*, on the other hand, hide behind pretense all the time. Even though they're entitled to hold any opinion for any reason, they pretend to be better than that. They like to believe that they actually keep an open mind on the controversial issues of the day, and reach their lofty conclusions only after careful deliberation of the facts. The deception may work on them, but it no longer works on the rest of us who understand all too well that they're just left-wing ideologues, as orthodox and doctrinaire in their views as any right-wing ideologue is in his.

So yes, the elites are different. And yes, Mr. Capone was right: They are quite good at hypocrisy—and blissfully shameless about it, too. Practice makes perfect, after all.

Letters
from the
Fringe

I love reading the letters to the editor in the
New York Times. The first thing I do when I look at the paper is
check to see what classified national-security secrets, the disclosure
of which might endanger American lives, the *Times* is plastering all
over the front page on this particular day. Then I scan the obituar-
ies to make sure I'm not one of them. Then it's right to the letters.

Reading these little gems is like taking a field trip to a mental
institution without having to worry that one of the patients might
get free and try to hurt you. It's really fun.

Many of the letters are about the previously mentioned "so-
called war on terror," which started arriving at the *Times* not long
after the "so-called" attack on the World Trade Center and the
Pentagon on September 11, 2001. But the letter writers have a vast
array of interests and so they write about all sorts of things.

For example, after Vice President Cheney accidentally shot a
hunting companion, there was a letter from Don in Olympia, Washington, who asked, "If we can't trust Mr. Cheney and company
with a simple shotgun, why should we trust them with this nation's
Defense Department?"

It's a very good question. Here's another: Are you aware, Don,
that some lunatic is writing letters to the *New York Times* and sign-
ing your name to them?

Then there were the letters compiled under the *Times* headline

"The Gloom Over This Presidency." David from the Bronx wanted to know "Which of Mr. Bush's failures this term could not have been predicted by his incompetence and arrogance in the first term? I propose that the answer is none . . ." So what does David think we should do about all those morons who voted for W. the second time around? They "should be apologizing," he says, "to those who knew better when it mattered most"—that is, *before* George W. Bush won reelection.

A very good idea! If you vote for the "incompetent" and "arrogant" winner why shouldn't you have to apologize to all the "smart" people who voted for the loser? Makes sense to me, though I'm not sure exactly how you would go about saying "I'm sorry" to 50 million people or so. But these are mere details.

Oh, and there was a nice letter from Mitchell who lives in the People's Republic of Palo Alto, about the "public hysteria over terrorism" in this country that "re-enacts the anti-Communist frenzy of the 1950s."

Thank you, Mitchell, for the information. Many of us who are rational did not know about the public hysteria you have detected; or the frenzy, either. I was surprised, however, that you left out the rumor that Bush and Cheney had hired Halliburton to build concentration camps for anyone who disagrees with them about anything.

But my favorite—at least until I open tomorrow's paper—is the one from Wilhemina in Seattle, who writes about those rules against bringing liquids and gels onto airplanes. Wilhemina points out that one airline spokesman, for a British carrier, had said his airline advised travelers to also put their *books* in checked luggage. This, she correctly points out, is nonsense. "The few seconds it takes to leaf through a book to check and see that it is not a hiding place for explosives seems well worth the time and effort." I completely agree! But then the lady from Seattle spots what may in fact be the *real* concern over bringing books on airplanes. "Unless, of course, it is the power of words and a literate populace that the government fears is dangerously subversive," she writes.

Of course! Why didn't I think of that? Never mind that the *government* didn't say you can't bring books on board; that an airline executive did—and a foreign one at that. Mere technicalities. This fear of books and ideas obviously is all part of the U.S. government's phony-baloney war on terrorism. Because, as Wilhemina wisely points out, if we read too much we might get smart and the government cannot allow anything as subversive as that to happen in the United States of America. Thank you very much, Wilhemina, for opening my eyes.

There is a serious point to be made about all this—about the aforementioned Bush derangement syndrome and liberal paranoia—but to be perfectly honest, I have no desire to make it. All I want is for the sufferers of BDS to keep writing. They amuse me. And since the *Times* doesn't have a funnies page, the letters section is the next best thing.

★ ★ ★ ★ ★ ★ ★ ★ ★ ★

My Plans to
Fix the World

My Plan to Fix Affirmative Action

I asked a young colleague once how he felt about diversity and affirmative action. Figuring he was a liberal, like just about everybody else in the media, I knew the answer before I asked. "I'm for it," he said.

"Good," I replied. "So would you give up *your* job so that a qualified minority or woman could have it?" He looked at me confused. No one had ever asked him such an odd question. He stammered all over the place and finally said, "But I *already* have the job," as if such a lame response would get me to change the subject.

"What about college admissions?" I asked him. "What if, in the name of diversity, you, a white kid, had been rejected in favor of another applicant, mainly because the other kid was a minority? Would that be okay with you?"

Again, despite the fact that he had gone to an Ivy League school, all I got was stammering before I let him off the hook and said, "Never mind."

I sympathize with my young colleague. He didn't make the rules. He's a good guy who wants everyone to have the same chance he did—at least in theory.

A few years earlier I put the same question to two friends, white, middle-aged men who were senior executives at two major American corporations. Both thought diversity was important in business and was also good for America (not to mention their careers). Both acknowledged they used race as a factor—often a major factor—in deciding who got hired and who got promoted.

"But if we do it your way," I told each of them in separate conversations, "it will take years and years to achieve the kind of racial equality you say you're looking for. My way will do it, literally, overnight."

"And exactly how would that work?" they asked in a tone suggesting they weren't really interested but were willing to humor me.

"Here's how," I said. And then I unveiled my plan.

"All you have to do," I told them, "is resign. Right now! And you do it on the condition that only a qualified minority or woman can take your place. What do you say?"

Like my young colleague, they were less than enthusiastic. And like my young colleague, they stammered all over the place but really said nothing; nothing except that you can't simply replace someone of their experience with a new person overnight. But, of course, you can—if you really want to.

But they don't really want to. They're for affirmative action—as long as it doesn't cost them anything. As I mentioned earlier, a lot of liberals are like that.

But if affirmative action and racial preferences are such a good idea, then why don't we use them in really important things, like sports and politics?

Let's start with basketball. To make college and pro teams more diverse, let's reject some really talented black players in favor of white guys, who might not be as good but bring something very important to the table—namely the color of their skin; their minority whiteness.

But what about merit, you say. Shouldn't we take the best players without regard to race? In a word, No! White kids grow up with a distinct disadvantage. They go to inferior high schools (basketball-wise), and could never compete in the big leagues without affirmative action.

But won't the white kids feel stigmatized? Won't they know they got picked for the team not because of their ability but because of their skin color? Who cares! Too much is at stake to worry about such insignificant matters. Sports, as we all know, are a microcosm of America. And so America has a stake in the greater good. And that greater good is called . . . diversity!

My plan is to initiate affirmative action at two college-basketball powerhouses: the University of Michigan and Michigan State. Why there? Because in 2006 the head coaches of the men's basketball teams at both those schools publicly came out against a state ballot measure that would have outlawed racial preferences in college admissions. "I know what it takes to build a team," Tom Izzo, the Michigan State coach said, "and that is diversity. We need all kinds of players on our team."

Silly me. I used to think that coaches like Tom Izzo recruited "all kinds of players" based on just one thing: ability! Now, I know better.

So, if Coach Tom Izzo and his pal Coach Tommy Amaker of the University of Michigan care so much about diversity then I'm sure they'd be very happy to ditch four or five of their talented black players to make room for four or five young white men who can't jump—or maybe can't dribble, either. All in the name of diversity, of course!

Now let's move on to politics. Under my plan, beginning with the 2008 presidential campaign, every white male candidate would have to tell the American people where he stands on affirmative action as it is currently practiced—meaning that race is used not just as *a* factor, but often as *the* factor in deciding who gets into college or who gets hired in the workplace. Once we've established who's for it and who's against it, we would then use the University of Michigan affirmative action plan as our model. Under that plan, certain applicants got twenty extra "admission points" simply because they were minorities. The system worked quite well. It kept many highly qualified white kids out, since they had the wrong skin color. Diversity, as we all know by now, is more important than anything else.

And so it is with presidential politics. Last time I checked, this country had never elected a black president. That's because Americans are racists. If they weren't, they would have elected a fine, decent, honorable man like Al Sharpton, when he ran.

Under my plan every white male candidate who comes out in favor of affirmative action—if he is running against a woman or a racial minority—would have to spot that candidate ten percentage points before the votes are even counted, to make up for past injustices against women and minorities. So if the white male candidate were to "win" the vote by, say, nine percentage points—he would in fact lose the election, because of the ten bonus points. What could be more fair?

I think my plan will make America a better place. Now, let the stammering begin.

My Plan for Peace in the Middle East

Since nobody else's so-called Roadmap for Peace in the Middle East has worked, why not give mine a try?

During the big flare-up in 2006, the pundits on television and in the press pointed out several key factors that contribute to endless tension and bloodshed between Arabs and Jews. If these obstacles could be overcome, they said, we might actually have peace in that part of the world. So I've outlined below the biggest problems in the Middle East today, as well as my proposed solution for each:

Problem #1: Whenever things heat up in the Middle East, more Arabs get killed than Israelis.

This, as we all know, is not fair. More Israeli civilians need to die if there is ever going to be peace in that part of the world. Yes, it's true that Arab civilians die in greater numbers than Israelis because the terrorists—Hezbollah in Lebanon and Hamas in Gaza—live in the same neighborhoods as non-combatant civilians; that they often live on the same block or even the same house; that sometimes they even sleep in the same bed. And yes, it's also true that Hezbollah actually pays rent to civilians who hide the terrorists' rockets and launchers in their houses, calling into question—only by cynics, of course—just how *civilian* these civilians really are.

But to any fair-minded person, these poor people are simply innocent victims of Israeli aggression. How are they supposed to know that Hezbollah is going to launch rockets into places like Haifa? They're not mind readers!

In any event, the disproportionate number of deaths among these innocent bystanders leads to anger and frustration on the always-reasonable and rational Arab Street, which, naturally, hinders the prospects for peace.

Solution: To achieve peace, Israel may shoot only at official card-carrying members of Hezbollah and Hamas who actually hold up their cards during battle, and only if they're actually in the process of trying to kill Israelis.

If there is any doubt about who's shooting at them, Israel must hold its fire. If the brave men of Hezbollah and Hamas, while hiding behind the skirts of old ladies, lob rockets into Israeli population centers, Israel must not respond. If this doesn't solve the problem of "disproportionality," as it's called, then Israeli soldiers must shoot and kill their fellow Israeli civilians in order to make the civilian death toll more equal. This eventually will lead to peace.

While they're at it, Israelis must also refrain from calling those who intentionally fire rockets into civilian neighborhoods "terrorists." One man's terrorist, after all, is another man's freedom fighter. Which is exactly why, as a matter of official state policy, Israel must start referring to the terrorists as "freedom fighters"—a description they prefer, and one that will surely put big smiles on their faces and encourage them *at long last* to lay down their arms and make peace with the Jewish state.

Problem #2: Israel relinquishes land for peace in order to instigate war.

It's true. Everyone knows that all the Arabs want is to live in peace, and that the official policy of the state of Israel is, instead, to wage relentless war against its Arab neighbors until every last one of them is driven into the sea—unless, of course, they don't have a sea, in which case the Israelis want to drive them someplace else that isn't particularly hospitable.

When Israel occupied Arab land—Gaza, for example, and southern Lebanon—Arabs fired hundreds of rockets into Israel to protest the occupation. Then when Israel withdrew from both Gaza and southern Lebanon, Arabs fired hundreds of rockets into Israel to underscore Israel's perceived weakness.

When will Israel stop provoking its neighbors?

Solution: Israel must not occupy one inch of Arab land— nor must it give back one inch of Arab land.

Both policies are provocative and intended to cause trouble.

Problem #3: Israel is a mistake that needs to be corrected.

Israel has no business being in the Middle East in the first place. Syndicated columnist Richard Cohen made this very point as the fighting was still raging in July 2006.

"The greatest mistake Israel could make at the moment is to forget that Israel itself is a mistake," Cohen wrote. "The idea of creating a nation of European Jews in an area of Arab Muslims (and some Christians) has produced a century of warfare and terrorism of the sort we are seeing now. Israel fights Hezbollah in the north and Hamas in the south, but its most formidable enemy is history itself."

Solution: Israel must cease to exist and all Israelis must leave the region.

Israelis must pack their bags and move. They must give

what we now call Israel over to the Arabs. The Israelis can go to Uganda, which has been suggested before. Or they can move to an uninhabited part of the Sahara Desert. Or they can move to the North Pole. Or they can move to Death Valley in the United States, though this is problematic, since the newly formed coalition of right-wing anti-Semites and left-wing anti-Semites probably would not approve of so many new Jews living in America.

So, as you can see, this is not going to be easy. But then, peace never comes easy. Still, as a first step, we must acknowledge that Israel is the real problem. It is a thorn in the side of civilized nations.

The idea of a strong Jew is unsettling to many. The very notion that Jews would be the toughest guys in the neighborhood, capable of kicking everybody else's ass, simply doesn't fit the template. And this becomes an obstacle to peace, too.

So the burden, as it should be, is on the Israelis. Get out of the Middle East—and the sooner the better. And if you don't fancy moving to Uganda or the Sahara or the North Pole or Death Valley, then I think the Jews should do what many have suggested they do for centuries. They should all go straight to hell. That will surely lead to peace in the Middle East.

My Plan to End Pork

And last, but certainly not least, here is my fabulous plan to stop the hogs in Washington from spending our hard-earned money on pork.

First you get two revolving drums, like the kind they used to use on those old TV game shows. In one drum you put the names of all one hundred U.S. senators, individually, on folded-over small pieces of paper. In the other drum you do the same with the names of all fifty states.

Then, broadcast to the entire nation on C-SPAN and the Game Show channel, you get Bob Barker from *The Price Is Right* to spin the drums. Round and round they go until all the pieces of folded paper are mixed up. Bob opens the door to the drum with the senators' names in it and picks out a piece of paper.

Bob looks at the name and reads it out loud. "Senator Ted Stevens," he would say, for example. Then, Bob would stick his hand in the other drum and pick out a state. "Florida," Bob might announce.

Here's where the brilliance of my plan begins to unfold. Stevens, you see, is the senator from Alaska. He's been the senator from Alaska since Moses was wearing short pants. Stevens is the one who spends gazillions of *your* tax money to bring the bacon home to Alaska. But why would he continue to do that if he represented Florida?

Think about it. If you live in Florida, do you really want *your* tax money to go for some "Bridge to Nowhere" in *Ketchikan*? Of course not! So why would the people of Alaska—the only ones who get to vote on whether Stevens stays in the Senate—want *their* tax money to go for an alligator museum in *Tampa*? In other words, what's in it for Stevens to dole out pork to Florida when Floridians can't do anything for him in return?

I know. I'm a genius.

Six years later, if Stevens is reelected by the voters in Alaska, Bob Barker would spin the drum again. Next time Stevens might represent Rhode Island, or California, or Texas. That way, he isn't in one place long enough to corrupt the whole damn system, as is now the case.

And here's another benefit my plan provides: If the only voters who can reelect you live in your old home state, maybe—just maybe—senators will start to act in the best interest of the *nation*, and not in the interest of some hack from back home who needs a monument in his district to please the boys down at the Chamber of Commerce.

The more I think about it the more I'm convinced that my plan to end pork is not only brilliant but also downright patriotic.

Okay, one senator down, ninety-nine to go. Bob Barker opens the drum door again, reaches in, and pulls out another name. This time he announces to the audience, "Robert C. Byrd"—a politician who, not for nothing, has been given the name "King of Pork" by Citizens Against Government Waste. You see, everything in West Virginia is named after Robert Byrd. Everything. And guess who paid for all of it? *You did!*

In case you're wondering just where your money went, here's a *very* short list of the pork Byrd brought home. There's the Robert C. Byrd Expressway, the Byrd Aerospace Tech Center, the Robert C. Byrd Federal Courthouse, the Robert C. Byrd Industrial Park, the Robert C. Byrd Institute for Advanced Flexible Manufacturing, the Robert C. Byrd Bridge, the Robert C. Byrd addition to the lodge at Oglebay Park, the Robert C. Byrd Library, the Robert C. Byrd Hilltop Office Complex, and about a million more Robert C. Byrd projects that would require a lot more pages to list.

Then Bob Barker would spin the other revolving drum, reach in, and this time come up with, say, "Wyoming"—which means that Robert C. Byrd, who used to represent West Virginia, would now be the U.S. senator from the great state of Wyoming, serving people who didn't vote for him and can't reelect him no matter how many Institutes for Advanced Flexible Manufacturing he builds with tax-payer money in Wyoming.

Senator Byrd, who was first elected to the Senate in 1958, has said that "West Virginia has always had four friends: God Almighty, Sears Roebuck, Carter's Liver Pills, and Robert C. Byrd." Now that he's representing Wyoming, make that three.

The drum spinning continues, and after all one hundred senators are assigned states, the whole process starts all over again, this time with Bob Barker reaching into the drums to assign members of the House of Representatives to districts in their brand-new states.

Bob Barker is our only hope. Spinning the drums is the only way to end the *porkidemic* of spending in Washington. Let's face it: Asking a politician to *voluntarily* stop spending our hard-earned money on crap is like asking a pig to vote for Jimmy Dean.

★ ★ ★ ★ ★ ★ ★ ★ ★ ★ ★

A Few Final
Words . . .

MoveOn.Jerk

On September 10, 2007, General David Petraeus, the commanding officer in charge of coalition forces in Iraq, testified before Congress on the progress of the war. That same day, MoveOn.org, the left-wing antiwar group, ran its now infamous full-page ad in the *New York Times*. "General Petraeus or General Betray Us?" the headline read. In the copy below, MoveOn said that the general was "constantly at war with the facts" and that he was "cooking the books for the White House."

There are many ways to call someone a liar, and those are two of them.

In the poisonous political climate that has taken over our culture, you can say just about anything about just about anybody and get away with it. Opponents aren't simply misguided or even just plain wrong these days. They're liars! And sometimes worse!

But to use the word "betray" against a military man who has dedicated his life to serving his country, crosses a very bright line—one that obviously didn't stand in the way of the left-wing partisans at MoveOn. Surely MoveOn knew that to a soldier, "betrayal" is a word that carries the stench of disgrace and dishonor. It suggests that General Petraeus was not only lying to the American people for political purposes, which is bad enough, but that he was betraying his country in the process.

I may be out of step with my fellow conservatives, but I would have been content to *briefly* denounce the ad—out of respect for the general and everyone else in the military, and out of common decency. I would have been more than willing to write it off as a dumb juvenile stunt. Rhyming names with bad words went out in the third grade anyway, didn't it? But the Democrats who want to be president—and *commander in chief*, might I add—managed to do something even dumber than what the name-callers at MoveOn did. *They refused to condemn the ad.* Every one of them kept mum, except Joe Biden, who had the guts to say, "I don't buy into that. This is an honorable guy." The rest ran for cover, proving—if any more proof is really needed—that today's Democrats are more afraid of offending left-wing activists in their party than they are of offending a four-star general, or anybody else in the United States military for that matter.

When Hillary Clinton was asked point blank by John Roberts on CNN whether she thought "that MoveOn.org ad [was] over the top," all she could muster in response was that she's a "strong admirer" of the general. That's nice. So why wouldn't she condemn the ad that suggested the very same general she so admires was a traitor?

On Fox News Sunday, it was the same song and dance. "This is not a debate about an ad," she told Chris Wallace. "This is a debate about the war in Iraq." Maybe Hillary was ready to move on, but John McCain, who had been following Hillary's remarks on the campaign trail, wasn't. "My conclusion," he said, "is that if you're not tough enough to take on MoveOn.org and their attacks on a decent and honorable member of the United States military, then you can't be tough enough to be president of the United States."

And when the United States Senate voted on a resolution to condemn the MoveOn ad—a resolution sponsored by Republicans trying to make the most of the Democrats' predicament—every Nay vote, twenty-five of them in all, came from Democrats, including two from Democrats who want to be president: Senators Clinton and Chris Dodd. Another Democratic senator and presidential wannabe, Barack Obama, not only refused to condemn the MoveOn ad when questioned by reporters, he refused to even cast a vote on the Senate resolution.

The American people are desperately looking for leadership, and this was a golden opportunity for Hillary and the other Democrats to step up to the challenge. All they had to do was say what so many Americans, no matter their politics, were saying: This is wrong! This is not how you treat an honorable man, a four-star general in the United States Army! But the Democrats just couldn't bring themselves to stand up to MoveOn, no matter how outrageous the smear.

Why? Because MoveOn is the Democratic Party's ATM, the cash machine that hands out oodles of money to sufficiently "progressive" Democrats, the powerful organization that helped the party take over Congress in 2006. It takes courage to stand up to your sugar daddy.

And this is the real disgrace of MoveOn's ad—not that it ran in the first place but that supposedly *mainstream* Democrats, politicians who want to be president, lacked the guts to stand up and denounce such a cheap and nasty political drive-by.

But rest assured the Republicans will not let voters forget how craven the Democratic candidates were back in September 2007—and how beholden they remain to MoveOn. This wasn't about the general's military strategy. This was about decency.

Because the war in Iraq is so unpopular, Americans may decide they've had enough, not just of George W. Bush but of the whole Republican Party. They may, in fact, be ready for a change. Another Clinton may be inaugurated president of the United States in January 2009.

But one thing is for sure: If the Democrats win the White House in 2008, MoveOn plans to have a great big seat at the table when all the important decisions are made—whether the topic is health care or foreign policy or domestic surveillance. MoveOn will be there for all of it. They've already told us as much.

After funneling millions into the John Kerry campaign and to the Democratic National Committee in 2004, Eli Pariser, the (then) twenty-four-year old political firebrand who runs MoveOn, put out a statement announcing that "grassroots contributors like us gave more than $300 million to the Kerry campaign and the DNC, and proved that the Party doesn't need corporate cash to be competitive." And then Pariser, speaking for "the whole MoveOn PAC team," put the final touch on his declaration, just in case some dim-witted Democrat didn't understand what he was really saying. "Now it's our Party," he said. "We bought it, we own it, and we're going to take it back."

MoveOn was wrong to run the "General Betray Us" ad. But they're right about something else: They did indeed buy the Democratic Party. They really do own it. And now it's theirs to do what they want with it.

Why the Crazies Are on Top (for Now)

By now we know why the Republicans got a thumpin' on Election Day 2006, to use President Bush's down-home word to describe the beating his party took: the war in Iraq, corruption, out-of-control spending, and the general perception that Republicans abandoned their principles—*that they sold out!* The Democrats pretty much ran on one big issue—the "We're Not Republicans" issue—and it was more than enough to win big, proving you really can beat something with nothing.

For months before the election, as I traveled around the country, I noticed something new. Something I hadn't picked up on before. Conservatives were getting angry—*with Republicans!* It began as a quiet rumble. But the rumble got louder the closer we got to Election Day. By the time the votes were in, the rumbling was a roar. The volcano had erupted.

One conservative I admire said, "There hasn't been any ideology in the Republican Party, any conservatism, for at least two to maybe four years. I've always believed that those of us who are conservative believe in the ideology. We believe it wins. We believe it's best for the country. We believe it's best for the people. We believe it's ultimately compassionate, and it has not been present."

The conservative was Rush Limbaugh. When *he* starts taking off on the Republicans, you know things are bad. "It isn't my job," Rush said, "to make elected Republicans look good if they can't do it themselves. It's not my job to make them understandable and understood if they can't do it themselves—not in perpetuity, not ad infinitum."

But we've got to give the Democrats *some* credit. They were smart enough to figure out that you really can fool some of the people all of the time—and those voters are the ones they decided to concentrate on. So, Nancy Pelosi, the liberal Democrat who would be the first woman Speaker of the House, went missing in the days leading up to the election, a good way to make sure those less sophisticated voters wouldn't notice how left-wing she is, which might have caused them to think twice before voting Democratic.

Word must have gone out to the Hollywood crowd, too, to put a sock in it, because none of the political geniuses on the Left Coast called Bush a moron or a Nazi even once as Election Day approached—not in public, anyway. The Democrats even ran a few candidates in red states who were against abortion and for guns, the kind of Democrat, in other words, who doesn't look anything like a Democrat.

The only screwup was letting John Kerry out of his padded cell. Kerry, you'll recall, botched his "joke" about how only stupid American kids who don't study hard wind up in uniform fighting in Iraq—and the Democrats put him into the Witness Protection Program for the duration of the campaign.

In other words, liberal Democrats pretended they weren't liberals and even without any new ideas about anything, they won.

And so in the weeks following the disastrous election, like a lot of others on the losing side, I started worrying that if these phonies can keep the charade going for a while they might actually win the White House in 2008.

But it won't be easy. Politicians, being the professionals that they are, may be able to keep the nasty stuff in check for a couple of years but it is a lot harder to keep the unruly rank and file in line during the long term. It took political scientist Danny DeVito—representing the always witty and sophisticated Hollywood community—just three weeks after the 2006 election to go on national television—*The View*—and call President Bush "numb nuts." A few weeks after that, again on *The View*, Joy Behar, one of the liberal cohosts of the show, compared Donald Rumsfeld to Hitler. And sooner or later (by the time you're reading this it may have already begun) left-wing intellectual elites will also revert to form and start chanting their old mantra about how Bush is a war criminal who must be impeached and how France does everything better than we do.

Liberals, after all, are liberals. Which means many of them will continue to support late-term abortion. Many will continue to rail against "oppressive" laws that force thirteen-year-old girls to actually inform their own parents before they get an abortion. Racial-grievance groups will continue to yell about racism in America. Feminists will continue to whine about the "male-dominated culture." And practically none of this will resonate with ordinary Americans—the ones who make up a majority of our country's citizens and live between Manhattan and San Francisco.

That's the good news. As Rush Limbaugh also said one day after the election: "You can always count on the Democrats, at some point, to revive conservatism in this country by being who they are."

He's right about that, of course. But the real question is: Will *Republicans* get back to being who they're *supposed to be*—principled and conservative?

In 1946, the GOP took control of Congress with the slogan "Had Enough?" In 2006, Democrats essentially ran with the same message, though they didn't actually use the words. And it worked, because Republicans had lost their souls long before they lost the midterm election. After they got routed, the conservative pundit

George Will had a good line: "At least Republicans now know where the 'Bridge to Nowhere' leads: to the political wilderness."

With the 2008 presidential election just around the corner, it might be a good idea for Republicans to take those words and paste them somewhere—on their office doors, perhaps. Or better yet, on their foreheads.

If the 2006 election taught the Republicans one thing—and the jury is out on whether it has—it is that if you're going to pretend to be the conservative party and make believe you stand for limited government while you're spending boatloads of taxpayer money on nonsense, if you're going to betray everything you supposedly stand for, the voters *will* notice and will realize that you stand for absolutely nothing. It may be true, to some extent anyway, that politics is the enemy of principle. But compromise is one thing; abandoning everything you believe in is something else altogether.

Republicans forgot who they were and what they believed in. All they cared about was staying in power. They thought they could buy voters off with taxpayer-funded pork, like that $223 million "Bridge to Nowhere," a piece of pork that came to symbolize all the other junk our tax dollars were being wasted on. They thought they could spend and spend and spend and in the process buy permanent control of Congress. And they thought they could get away with it all simply because they weren't Democrats!

Well, they were wrong. Republicans lost, and as far as I'm concerned they deserved to lose. No one respects a panderer. When voters say they believe *Democrats* are the "small government" party, which is exactly what they said in 2006, you know something has gone terribly wrong.

But before the Democrats start measuring the drapes in the Oval Office, they might want to consider some other news that didn't get a whole lot of play in the aftermath of the last election—news that shows that while *Republicans* are on the ropes, *conservative* ideas are still very much alive and well.

Consider this:

In California, four ballot measures that would have raised taxes, in a state that is already overtaxed, went down to defeat.

Seven states—including liberal Wisconsin and conservative South Dakota—passed ballot measures banning same-sex marriage.

And perhaps the most significant victory for conservative values came in Michigan, where voters overwhelmingly (58 percent to 42 percent) passed an initiative to outlaw racial preferences. The initiative simply said that "The State shall not discriminate against, or grant preferential treatment to any individual or group on the basis of race, sex, color, ethnicity, or national origin in the operation of public employment, public education or public contracting." As the *Wall Street Journal* put it, "One might think a law banning discrimination would be a triumph for civil rights." But when it comes to racial preferences, one might have to think again.

So, who were the opponents of Proposal 2, as the ballot measure was called? Well, the Democrats, of course. But they were not the only ones. Just about every important Republican in Michigan came out against Proposal 2 also, including the Republican candidates for governor and senator. While the anti-preference measure won big, they both lost big—just like a lot of other Republicans around the country who thought they were playing it safe by downplaying, if not entirely abandoning, their conservative principles.

Yes, it's true the Republican Party got drubbed on Election Day 2006. But conservative values didn't. So what happened? Democrats in Congress, in power for the first time in a long time, managed to alienate just about everyone in no time flat—starting with the perpetually angry left-wing base of their own party, which blamed them for not stopping the war in Iraq the day before yesterday. The fact is, most Democrats would love to shut down the war but don't have the guts to cut off funding for the troops, knowing that would only feed into their well-deserved reputation for being soft on national security. And how would that play in an election year? So they mumbled and grumbled and pretty much got nothing done, still figuring they'd win back the White House. Given W's unpopularity, they may be right.

But an optimistic Republican who speaks with moral clarity and eloquence can rebuild the coalition that began to fall apart in 2006, and put the disparate elements of the party back together: the small-government conservatives, men, married women, parents, evangelicals, Catholics.

Great leaders have managed to hold disparate factions together before. Franklin Roosevelt did. He had northern liberals and southern conservatives on his side, communists and segregationists—factions that had virtually nothing in common and detested each other to boot.

Reagan did it, too. "A political party cannot be all things to all people," he said in the 1970s, before he won the GOP nomination and became president. "It must represent certain fundamental beliefs which must not be compromised to political expediency, or simply to swell numbers. This is the very basis of conservatism." This kind of talk drew voters from vastly different backgrounds, voters who elected him with huge majorities. Sure, leftists on college campuses, liberals in Hollywood, and a lot of journalists thought he was a cowboy, a warmonger, and an "idiot actor," but all sorts of other Americans idolized him. He was a hero on Wall Street, of course; but Americans earning between $25,000 and $50,000 a year loved him, too. Independents were drawn to him. Even disillusioned "life-long" Democrats became enthusiastic Reagan supporters.

All of these disparate groups understood that this was a man not just with a sunny disposition—which, after Jimmy Carter, Mr. Malaise himself, was a welcome relief—but that this was that rare politician who actually believed in something. By being himself, Ronald Reagan built a Republican coalition that lasted some thirty years, until pandering became the party's guiding principle, and the coalition began to unravel.

In 1994, Republicans took over Congress for the first time in forty years and came up with their "Contract with America" that vowed to shrink the size of government, to balance the budget, to end the "cycle of scandal and disgrace" in Congress. By 2006, it was painfully obvious that they had violated the contract and broken their promises. They pandered so much that it finally caught up with them.

So now it's pretty simple: Republicans need to get back to basics. They need to start thinking and acting like real conservatives again—instead of behaving like cynical politicians who thought they could win by rising above their principles. If they do, then the crazies on the Left may not be on top for long. But if they don't, the Republicans could very well remain the minority party for a long, long time.

So, conservatives can take stock now, or else they'll have plenty of time for introspection later, after the big-goverment, high-taxing, soft-on-national-security liberal Democrat is sworn in. If that thought depresses you, be assured it depresses me also.

But here's the good news: As the brilliant Israeli statesman Abba Eban famously said of the Arabs, "They never miss an opportunity to miss an opportunity."

Same with the Democrats!

Could they possibly have had a better opportunity for a long-term lease on 1600 Pennsylvania Avenue than after Richard Nixon resigned in disgrace? Could things possibly have been brighter for them? And what do they do? They give us Jimmy Carter. Which led, just four years later, to Ronald Reagan and the revival of conservatism in America.

The question now isn't whether the Democrats will miss another opportunity to miss an opportunity. The question is whether Republicans will *seize* the opportunity. Will they remember who they're supposed to be? Will they embrace the "fundamental beliefs which must not be compromised to political expediency" that Ronald Reagan talked about?

The question, in plain English, is: Will they "Man Up!"?

Acknowledgments

This book would not have been possible were it not for all the crazy liberals who provided me with so much ammunition to use against them. You know who you are. Thank you.

A big thank-you, too, to the many despicable sellouts on the Right—those gutless wonders who care more about staying in power than standing up for their principles. Without their cowardice, I would never have decided to write this book.

And a tip of the hat to several good guys: my first-class editor, Kate Hamill, and my copy editor, Olga Gardner Galvin, who both asked the right questions, which helped me focus and strengthen my arguments. Their intelligence, substantial as it is, will not be enough, of course, to convince the crazies or the wimps that I'm right. Fortunately, I can live with that.

I would also like to acknowledge a debt of gratitude to several friends: John and Debbie Freud, who, as we talked about this book, thought I was on to something important; Gary Pollack and Tracy Wright, two (hopeless) liberals who frequently told me to stop writing and check myself into an asylum; and Harry Stein and Priscilla Turner, the two most knowledgeable people I know when it comes to deciphering American culture.

Let me also say a few words about my friends at the William Morris Agency—Jim Griffin and Mel Berger—who when I once

ALSO AVAILABLE BY
BERNARD GOLDBERG

CRAZIES TO THE LEFT OF ME, WIMPS TO THE RIGHT

How One Side Lost Its Mind and the Other Lost Its Nerve

978-0-06-125258-7 (pb) • 978-0-06-143561-4 (unabridged cd)

More hard-hitting observations and no-nonsense advice for saving America from the lunatics on the left and the sellouts on the right.

"Priceless...he takes on both sides as only a former member of the mainstream media can."
—*U.S. News & World Report*

110 PEOPLE WHO ARE SCREWING UP AMERICA

(and Al Franken Is #37)

978-0-06-076129-5 (pb) • 978-0-06-112653-6 (cd)

The instant *New York Times* bestseller that took the country by storm and pointed fingers at the 100 people who are helping to destroy the culture of America, now fully revised in paperback, with an updated introduction and 10 new names!

BIAS

A CBS Insider Exposes How the Media Distort the News

978-0-06-052084-7 (pb)

"*Bias* should be taken seriously....Mr. Goldberg has done real homework." —*New York Times*

"This insider's account...is filled with so many stories of repulsive elitism and prejudice on the part of his peers that it elevates *Bias* to must-read status."
—*Wall Street Journal*